SEASONS
of
INTERCESSION

God's Call to
Prayer-Intercession
for Every Believer

FRANK DAMAZIO

BT PUBLISHING
Portland, Oregon USA

Published by BT Publishing
9200 NE Fremont
Portland, Oregon 97220

Printed in U.S.A.

BT Publishing is a ministry of Bible Temple, and is dedicated to serving the
local church and its leaders through the production and distribution of quality
restoration materials.

It is our prayer that these materials, proven in the context of the local church,
will equip leaders in exalting the Lord and extending His kingdom.

*For a free catalog of additional resources from BT Publishing please call
1-800-777-6057 or visit our web site at www.btpublishing.com.*

ISBN 1-886849-08-0 - HC
ISBN 1-886849-11-0 - SC

Unless otherwise noted, all Scripture references are taken from the
New King James Version of the Bible.

With study questions contributed by Mike Balyo.

Dedication

I wish to dedicate this book to the many prayer warriors who have quietly, without reward or recognition, changed the course of people's lives, churches, cities and nations by digging in and stubbornly holding their ground through prayer-intercession. Without their dedication, discipline and determination, the church could never reach its true calling. Thank God for these warriors in every town, village, countryside, and city. Although in prisons, hospitals and other difficult circumstances, they remain true to the highest calling–prayer-intercession.

Table of Contents

Foreword by Ted Haggard
Preface: My Personal Journey Into Prayer-Intercession
Introduction

Appendix

Foreword
Seasons of Intercession
by Pastor Ted Haggard, New Life Church, Colorado Springs, Colorado

This is the season for intercession. As you read this book, you will receive some of the best practical information available on the role and effectiveness of prayer. Two years ago, I met Pastor Frank Damazio in a pastor's meeting at City Bible Church (formerly Bible Temple). I could immediately tell that he understood the spiritual nuances necessary for successful Christian living. In this book, the subtle distinctions that separate genuine and effective prayer from myths regarding prayer are beautifully articulated so that any seeking Christian can become the powerhouse of prayer that God desires.

Currently, the Body of Christ worldwide is growing at a rate of over 9% a year—three times the rate of our global population. Meanwhile, Islam is growing globally at a rate slightly over 2% a year. Those growth rates are encouraging, however, they are not reflective of the situation in North America. In North America, the Body of Christ has not enjoyed notable growth in over 20 years. On the other hand, Islam is gaining rapid acceptance in many cities. What's the difference? There are many, however, one obvious one is that Christians throughout the world are embracing intercessory prayer as a way of life and experiencing powerful growth, while Christians in North America still view intercession as a nice thing to do, but not a necessity for survival.

In October of 1993, the United Prayer Track of the AD2000 movement asked Christians all over the world to pray for the 62 countries of the 10/40 Window. To the surprise of Christian leaders worldwide, over 21,000,000

Christians from over 100 nations agreed to intercede daily for revival in these spiritually needy countries. That prayer effort has become known as *Prayer Through the Window I*.

Then in October of 1995, the United Prayer Track asked Christians to pray for the 100 gateway cities of the 10/40 Window, knowing that God wanted to touch entire populations of cities with His glory. In response to that request, over 36,000,000 intercessors from over 120 nations prayed every day for a month for revival in these strategic cities. That was *Prayer Through the Window II*.

We have just completed *Prayer Through the Window III* in October 1997. This effort networked Christians world-wide to pray for the 1,739 least evangelized people groups in the world. We have not been able to document how many people prayed during the month of October, but estimates range from 40 to 60 million intercessors!

Each of these prayer efforts staggered the projections of missions experts because no one ministry has ever been able to coordinate so many intercessors on behalf of the lost of the world. Not only have these efforts focused more attention on the lost, but each effort has also been followed with notable spiritual activity throughout the 10/40 Window. Just as one example, since the prayer effort began in 1994 the body of Christ in the Buddhist Kingdom of Nepal has doubled every year. Not all of the nations within the 10/40 Window have enjoyed this explosive growth, but all have experienced substantive spiritual activity–largely because of intercessory prayer.

These and other prayer efforts are more quickly embraced in other countries then in North America for a reason. We do not think we need prayer-intercession; we do not think it is necessary for survival! The Spirit of God though is changing us–and He is using books like this to do it. Seasons of Intercession addresses our passive comfort by moving us off center with practical application of prayer and it's associated opportunities through fasting. Seasons of Intercession is the premier text for the believer wanting to understand dynamic prayer. It's a book of eternal truths for this season, this *Season of Intercession*.

Preface:
My Personal Journey Into Prayer-intercession

The prayer coming from the old wooden pulpit had a sound of desperation to it. It was very sincere and emotional. The tears of the man praying flowed freely, without embarrassment. He was on his hands and knees, his tears falling onto the carpet. This was my first remembrance of my father, a Baptist pastor, doing what he called "the prayer of intercession." I did not understand it, but I felt it. I was only a young boy, but it moved something inside me.

The woman was a Bible teacher and prayer-intercessor. Her invitation to me and to one other young man was to join her and her husband on a prayer-intercession retreat in the mountains. We agreed. What we did not know was that we would be the only two going with them! Outside, winter snow fell heavily as we sat at a large bay window, studying the Bible and praying. I was not ready for the intensity, the boldness of asking such specific things, the length of time we spent in prayer (one hour, two hours, three hours). Praying in such a fashion was a first for me as a young, seventeen-year old "Jesus freak."

We learned together the power of worship and prayer, praying through the Psalms (all of them!) and praying through the book of Revelation (this was really interesting, especially some of our inspired interpretations!). I learned that the more time you spend in prayer, the more you want to spend. Time itself stops. I was introduced to the burden of prayer, the burden of interceding for others. It was so real, so spiritually life-changing that we came home different than we were when we left. I was marked, captured by this new desire to improve my prayer-intercession ability.

The group of young men sat on the floor as we studied Isaiah 58 together. The subject: prayer and fasting. The Albie Pearson Youth Foundation had provided these new converts with a house–a discipleship/prayer house. God was doing some awesome things in the youth of Riverside, California, through a major-league baseball player named Albie Pearson.

As we studied Isaiah 58, one of the new converts piped up, "Hey, why don't we try this fasting stuff?" We all responded with, "Right, okay. How? When? What do you do?" I had never willingly fasted unto God one day in my life. Within hours we were on our way to experience a three-day fast in the high desert, with Bibles, water bottles, blankets and a map to a desert cabin owned by a friend. We learned how to fast and pray by just sitting on the floor, reading our Bibles all day–literally, with each person taking thirty minutes to an hour–and then praying. I was not prepared for the presence of God in that little shack of a cabin. The Holy Spirit would come in waves. Prayers were prayed that sounded like something straight from heaven. It was marvelous, life-changing, difficult to stop. I learned that fasting and prayer combined caused a Kingdom explosion. Prayer-intercession came naturally. The burden to pray was strong, enduring and very real. I wanted more tutoring, more mentoring. I wanted more of this prayer-intercession spirit.

We had gathered in the basement of our house, mostly young couples and college-age students. Our project was to pray and plant a church in Eugene, Oregon. This was a serious moment in our lives. I was leaving my teaching position at Portland Bible College, where I had served for five years. That was home. Friends, security and a part of my ministry identity were attached to a thriving school and church. Now I was leaving, full of anticipation, vision–and natural apprehension. As we prayed, I shared what the Lord had impressed upon me in my days of fasting and prayer. It was the intercession during the time of fasting that had given me the confidence to plunge into the future with this small church plant team.

"Then I proclaimed a fast there at the river of Ahava, that we might humble ourselves before our God, to seek from Him the right way for us and our little ones and all our possessions. For I was ashamed to request of the king an escort of soldiers and horsemen to help us against the enemy on the road, because we had spoken to the king, saying, 'The hand of our God is upon all those for good who seek Him, but His power and

His wrath are against all those who forsake Him.' So we fasted and entreated our God for this, and He answered our prayer" (Ezra 8:21-23).

Prayer-intercession and fasting launched our church plant. Prayer-intercession and fasting established our church and became the pillar of strength in everything we did. Establishing a prayer-intercession foundation was the wisest step we took. We made no major moves without prayer and fasting.

After twelve years of pioneering and pastoring our church in Eugene, we left to return to our home church in Portland. We left a healthy church with some 1,200 people. We had planted several other churches, sent missionaries, bought and paid for 21 acres, built a beautiful complex and left with everything basically debt-free. This church is still healthy, growing under strong progressive leadership and is going on to fulfill greater vision.

The return to our home church (a mother church of some 45 churches and birthplace of a fellowship called Ministers Fellowship International with over 750 ministries), was the hardest and most important decision of our ministry. I was leaving a young church of twelve years to become pastor of a forty-five-year old church, one in which I had spent my formative years from age twenty to thirty. I needed more than an invitation, more than natural reasoning; I needed a God-word. My wife and I desperately needed God's divine guidance.

The prayer-intercession principle with fasting was tapped into once again. Many intercessors prayed with us. In times of great decision, making it takes great prayer and great pray-ers. Intercession is the road to the heart and the mind of God. After several months of wrestling, God came through loud and clear during prayer time, in the atmosphere of intercession.

The outpouring of God's grace and presence upon our church in Portland was apparent. It was not humanly hyped-up or humanly initiated. We were hungry for revival, for more of God's presence to be released in our church. We were aware of revival fires burning in many different places around the world–Canada, Brazil, Argentina, China, Russia, other places in the United States. Our attitude was one of "Oh God, please don't pass us by. If there is a genuine revival happening around the world, allow our church and our city to be involved." We initiated several forty-day periods of fasting and prayer for the whole church. We had a white board marked off into blocks for each of the forty days. The church members were encouraged to pick one day a week, two days a week, three days a week, whatever they could do. We logged over three thousand fasting days during the first fast. We also promoted our January prayer conference to wait on God with fasting and prayer. Intercession was made morning, noon and night.

God heard and responded to our intercession. A fresh, new attitude was shaped in the church, an attitude of spiritual hunger and a passion for God's presence. More people were saved in one year than in the previous several years, financial giving grew, new ministries were born. We added a downtown young adults outreach, a new Saturday night service and a new Prayer Center that is open seven days a week on our campus. I was impressed by the Holy Spirit to teach, preach, and nurture prayer until it was truly birthed in every person and the whole church moved into another level of prayer, especially prayer-intercession. This journey in the pulpit lasted over twelve months, but the results were obvious signs of a God-witness.

With the revival spirit catching fire in our church and nation, prayer-intercession was the natural response. Prayer, fasting and prayer-intercession are being preached, written about and taught in conferences and seminars worldwide. The pastors I meet around the world are very responsive to the subject of prayer-intercession, which is further evidence of a supernatural hunger worldwide.

In 1997, I was at a conference in England with three thousand people, four hundred of whom were pastors from all over Europe. There was an atmosphere of intense hunger and an obvious, lavish love for God. When I introduced my subject of prayer-intercession as "Gap Standing, Hedge Building and Cup Filling," the place erupted with shouts of praise and moved into a roar of prayer. It was an awesome experience to hear the sound of many waters as the voices rose loudly and fervently in prayer. What a day! What an experience!

Our Journey into Prayer-Intercession

Our journey into prayer-intercession will provide a basic, biblical perspective on prayer and intercession. Myths and misunderstandings about intercessory prayer will be replaced by basic truths. We will define the work of intercession, and then move into the function of intercession. Key intercessory Scriptures will be discussed, beginning with Ezekiel 22:30, the pilot text for major truths about intercessory prayer. Gap standing, hedge building and cup filling will be images to explain and to apply in the life of every praying Christian.

This journey will teach us how to stand in the gap for a nation and a generation and will outline the five goals of biblical intercession. We will examine the power of fasting with Holy Spirit-empowered intercession. Principles of prayer-intercession will be applied in workable and practical ways so all believers may learn and practice the prayer of intercession.

Intercessory prayers of adoration, confession, restitution, thanksgiving, forgiveness, faith, unity, supplication, submission, confidence, persistence, warfare, breakthrough: we will explore all of these areas as we examine prayer-intercession.

People are falling in love with prayer-intercession. All races, colors, sizes, denominations, male and female, young and old-there is a worldwide army of intercessors arising. This book is directed toward this groundswell, toward this revival of intercessory prayer. I am praying that you will catch the fire. I am praying that you—dear brother, sister, pastor, leader, businessman or woman—will let this message about prayer-intercession be imparted into your spirit, and that your life will be changed forever. (See Hebrews 4:16; 10:19; Daniel 11:32; John 14:12-14; I Chronicles 16:11.)

PRAYER

Father God, I come humbly to Your throne, through the blood of Jesus and by the Spirit of God. I bring specific petitions before You, petitions bathed in fasting and prayers. Oh God, invade, intercept every believer with a passion for prayer-intercession, a passion for gap standing and hedge building. Oh God, come arrest a generation for prayer-intercession, a generation of intercessors with a divine determination to stand in the gap for all people until we see an authentic revival in every nation of the world.

Introduction
Seasons of Intercession

As this book is written, the world is experiencing a global prayer awakening. This spirit of prayer is sweeping every country of the world that has a hunger for and openness to the Holy Spirit. It is no exaggeration to state that this prayer revival has the potential of seeing the Holy Spirit power, recorded in the book of Acts, restored in double portion. Revival news is reported from around the globe, with staggering statistics of thousands coming to Christ, of miracles, healing and other phenomena taking place.

Dr. C. Peter Wagner states in his book, *Churches That Pray*, "A prayer movement that greatly surpasses anything like it in living memory, perhaps in all of Christian history, is rapidly gaining momentum. In all the years I have ministered to pastors across America, I have never seen prayer so high on their collective agendas."[1] Dozens of prayer ministries are springing up all over North America and around the world. Some of these ministries only last for a few years, but others endure, among them Cindy Jacobs' *Generals of Intercession*, David Bryant's *Concerts of Prayer*, Esther Ilniskey's *Esther Network International*, Gary Bergel's *Intercessors for America*. Right here in my hometown of Portland, Oregon, Dr. Joseph Aldrich's *Prayer Summits* began and are now being held in over 200 cities in America alone! We are also aware of the World Prayer Center being built in Colorado Springs by the *A.D. 2000 and Beyond* movement, directed by Dr. C. Peter Wagner. Prayer is springing up everywhere and anywhere people have an ear to hear what the Spirit of God is saying.

Bill Bright's book, *The Coming Revival: America's Call to Fast, Pray and Seek God's Face*, has served as a powerful wake-up call for prayer-intercession leading to revival. Bill Bright's opening statement is bold, unheard of just a few short years ago: "To all believers who will join with me in fasting and praying for revival in North America and the fulfillment of the Great Commission around the world, especially to the two million for whom God has impressed me to pray who will fast forty days . . ."[2]

This call to fasting and prayer for forty days has been answered. Everywhere I go, people are fasting for forty days–housewives, blue collar workers, businesspeople, secretaries, students, ministers. In our church alone, more than fifteen people have chosen to fast and pray for forty days. With 330,000 churches in America, the results from such dedication should be awesome.

A few years ago, I had the privilege of personally attending a conference with David Yonggi Cho. One of his statements has remained with me ever since, stinging my conscience. He stated that in America he found the churches to be excellent in management, administration and music, but very poor in prayer. In Korea the pastors pray two to four hours a day and see great results. In America we sing, manage and administrate–often with very poor results.

What a challenge! But the Holy Spirit is on a mission of prayer revival. Wayman Rudges states, "The ministry of prayer is the most important of all the ministries in the church. Prayer creates the atmosphere and binds the powers of darkness so the gospel of Jesus can go forward."[3]

FEW AGONIZERS

Many organizers, few agonizers
Many players and payers, few prayers
Many singers, few clingers
Many pastors, few wrestlers
Many fears, few tears
Much fashion, little passion
Many interferers, few intercessors
Many writers, but few fighters

MISSION STATEMENT

Through this book I am hoping to add spiritual momentum to the prayer revival. My desire is to:

- **Inform using biblical research, spiritual insights, and practical keys for prayer-intercession.**
- **Inspire the reader's heart toward prayer-intercession through the Word of God, stories, principles, and prayer models.**
- **Impart the seeds of God's Word concerning prayer-intercession that will produce a great harvest.**
- **Impact each and every person with a vision to change cities, nations and history through prayer-intercession.**
- **Influence every believer toward the type of prayer which stands in the gap and builds hedges for our families, our churches, our cities, and our nations.**
- **Increase the faith of every believer to understand and utilize prayer as a powerful weapon to bring down spiritual strongholds and, thus reap an awesome harvest of souls.**
- **Intercept every open-hearted believer, both young and old, and yoke him or her to a Holy Spirit calling to intercede daily.**

As we develop the theme of intercessory prayer, we will work from some obvious presuppositions.

SEVEN BASIC PRESUPPOSITIONS ABOUT INTERCESSORY PRAYER:

1. Intercessory prayer is found in Scriptures, from Genesis to Revelation, as a definite kind of prayer to which God responds.
2. Intercessory prayer is demonstrated by many of God's chosen leaders, who practiced the ministry of intercession with awesome results (i.e., Job, Abraham, Isaac, Joseph, Moses, Esther).
3. Intercessory prayer was a prayer commitment of the first apostles, the first disciples, and the first church.
4. Intercessory prayer was, and is, the chief ministry of our Lord Jesus Christ, who is the mediator between God and man, and is presently the intercessor for man.
5. Intercessory prayer is the responsibility of every church that is ruled by Christ and His Word.
6. Intercessory prayer is being restored to the Church worldwide with what might be the greatest single emphasis since the first church in the book of Acts.
7. Intercessory prayer is a call of the Spirit to every believer now – today – in order to take back our cities, our regions, our nations, and our world for the Kingdom of God.

I will use Scripture to show how every believer is called to intercessory prayer. Some will give themselves to it more than others, but all will receive the invitation to make a difference through intercessory prayer. In this book, I plan to use every godly means possible to motivate every believer to embrace prayer-intercession. This is the time, we are the people and prayer is the force.

During the Second World War, Winston Churchill, then Prime Minister of Great Britain, set out to "win with words" over Hitler by raising the morale of the nation. Not only did he visit troops and factories, but he also went to the out-of-the-way coal-mining towns. On one visit to the hardworking coal miners, the Prime Minister urged them to see their significance in the total effort for victory. He told them, "We will be victorious! We will preserve our freedom. And years from now when our freedom is secure and peace reigns, your children and children's children will come, and they will say to you, 'What did you do to win our freedom in the Great War?' And one will say, 'I marched with the Eighth Army!' Someone else will proudly say, 'I manned a submarine.' And another will say, 'I guided the ships that moved the troops and supplies.' And still another will say, 'I doctored the wounds!' Then the great statesman paused. The dirty-faced miners sat in silence and awe, waiting for him to proceed. 'They will come to you,' he shouted, 'and you will say, with equal right and equal pride, "I cut the coal! I cut the coal that fueled the ships that moved the supplies! That's what I did. I cut the coal!" ' "[4]

Let us as responsible believers "cut the coal" for the church in these momentous days by fueling her with intercessory prayer.

Notes

1. Dr. C. Peter Wagner, Churches That Pray, (Ventura, CA: Regal Books), 17-18.

2. Bill Bright, The Coming Revival: America's Call to Fast, Pray and Seek God's Face, 1995.

3. Wayman Rudges, The Seed of Prayer in Church Growth, Church Growth, 1987, 19.

4. David Shibley, A Force in the Earth, 164.

The Scene
An Urgent Cry for Intercessors

Chapter One:
A Season for Intercession

The moon becomes very cold at night, even at the balmy lunar equator. Nighttime temperatures plunge to -143° Celsius. But by noon, temperatures jump to 127° Celsius, hotter than boiling water. Those frigid nights and scorching days drag on. Each lasts about one earth week long. And forget about waiting for summer or winter to roll around. The moon has no seasons. Aren't seasons a wonderful gift? I am glad I live on earth!

Seasons of life, seasons of nature, or spiritual seasons in the Church are all recognized and accepted as inevitable. The word "season" is synonymous with time. Seasons bring a sense of change, newness and excitement. Webster's dictionary speaks of seasons as "a set or suitable time, a time distinguished from others." To be in season is to be in good time or sufficiently early for the purpose. To be out of season is to be late, beyond the proper time, beyond the usual, appointed time.

Charles Swindoll, in his book, *Growing Strong in Seasons of Life*, states it perfectly: "Each of the four seasons offers fresh and vital insights for those who take the time to look and to think. Hidden beneath the surface are colorful yet silent truths that touch most every area across the landscape of our lives. As each three-month segment of every year holds its own mysteries and plays its own melodies, offering insights, smells, feelings, fantasies altogether distinct, so it is in the seasons of life."[1]

Seasons add spice to life. As we enjoy winter, spring, summer and fall (in most parts of the world) in the natural, so we embrace the seasons of God in the spiritual. As the natural climate changes, the atmosphere and attitude of people change with the season. We move from winter with its cold, short days and long nights, bare trees and somber shades, into spring with its glorious array of color. In my region, the Pacific Northwest, spring is an awesome time of year. Prior to it I begin to long for sunshine, blooming flowers, budding trees, a different atmosphere and a different attitude. Spring arrives suddenly, but the "suddenly" was so long in arriving! Springtime is filled with the message of resurrection, hope, renewal and starting over again. I love springtime!

Then summer! It is time to take a break, change my schedule, plan a family vacation, wear different clothes. By the time May is over, we have had many school events, with graduations at our elementary school, junior-high school, high school and college. There are special family events, staff gatherings, speaking engagements, awards and degree ceremonies. The Institute of Leadership Development at our church, a weeklong conference with an intense schedule, takes place at this time. Why do I do this to myself?!

When June arrives, I am ready for a definite change of pace and change of schedule. This is a refueling season for me. Office time is minimal and family time takes precedence. Traveling and speaking engagements are almost nonexistent. This is my "catch my breath" season, to get ready for the fall. Usually, by the end of summer I am ready to start my engine, ready to pull into the fast lane again. My wife is usually more than ready. Our four kids have drained her of most of her sanity, and she is ready for school.

What is our season? What should we be gaining from this appointed?

Fall hits with a bang. The whole church starts up, the schools, the college, the educational and youth activities. Off we go! I love it! I love fall! The Northwest fall is spectacular, the beauty of changing colors magnificent. Autumn brings cooler air, chilly nights, lit fires in the fireplace, warm sweaters, hot coffee. It is a busy time, full of challenges. Fall is my kind of season!

What would we do without seasons? The church also goes through its winters, springs, summers and falls. The Bible exhorts us to know our seasons, to be sensitive and discerning so we may gain all from each season.

What time is it now? What is our season? What should we be gaining from this appointed time?

Our Call to God's Appointed Seasons

The Apostle Paul instructed the Thessalonian church to understand the spiritual times and the seasons. He says in I Thessalonians 5:1, "But concerning the times and the seasons, brethren, you have no need that I should write to you." *New Testament Commentary*, by William Hendricksen, reads, "Now concerning the duration-periods and the appropriate seasons, brothers, you have no need that anything be written to you."

As believers, we are exhorted by Scripture to discern the approach of seasons of God, spiritually and historically. God has set out His appointed times and special seasons according to His divine purposes. Ecclesiastes 3:1 says, "To everything there is a season, a time for every purpose under heaven." From the beginning of time, God has proclaimed His purposes through the Scripture, through His covenants, His prophets and His apostles.

The dominant concern of Jesus during His earthly ministry was the Kingdom of God, and the mission to which He called His people is best understood in Kingdom terms. (See Matthew 4:17, 23; 11:12; Mark 1:14; Acts 20:25; 28:23, 31; Hebrews 12:28; Revelation 11:15.) Christ inaugurated and described this Kingdom, then demonstrated and exemplified it in His person and work. He gave to His people a model capable of infinite variation and amazing adaptability. The purpose of God in Christ was, and still is, to establish Christ's Church, to extend the Kingdom of God to all nations of the world. Each local church must grasp its role and place in the Kingdom.

The Church is the result of God's purpose and is the means for achieving that purpose. The Church has the same goal that God has: to reconcile persons to Himself and to restore lives to working order so as to be in harmony with His design. (See Romans 8:18-21; II Peter 3:13; I Corinthians 15:24; Colossians 1:28.)

> ## God's purpose is to change our cultures by the Kingdom of God.

God's purpose is to change our cultures by the Kingdom of God. When the opposite occurs, when Christianity is deeply influenced and infiltrated by our worldly culture, the true power of the gospel is neutralized. God's purpose is to recruit people from the world to become part of *Christ's* community, and to equip and mobilize these people to live and function, both in their local churches and in their particular world environment. God's purpose is for the Church to take the gospel to every person, to every tribe, to every nation!

It is rather strange that over the centuries the Protestant theological understanding of the Church's mission has rarely gone beyond defining the Church. Her mission to the nations has been only vaguely defined. Reformation did not take us far enough; the reformers failed in the articulation of the greater mission. The Church instead became bogged down with scholasticism, with a loss of vitality and real passion for the nations. The global mission was largely ignored.

Today we are experiencing a continued reformation because of the revival spirit. This is a special time and a divine season for the Church to fulfill God's mission and purpose. God, by His Spirit, is breathing life into His Church worldwide. It is vital for all of God's people to intercede in prayer for the advancement of Christ's Kingdom. God desires all of us to be mighty in prayer, experienced in getting prayer answers to even the most complex or seemingly impossible needs. We live in the glorious "now" of God, the season of Holy Spirit visitation, the season of global revival, the season of a global harvest of souls. Nations are being shaped by the gospel of Christ. This is a special and unique season of God, and we are in it!

Prayer-intercession is vital to the understanding of times and seasons.

The entire time of history has been God's arena to work on behalf of and through His faithful prayer-intercessors. God has promised His rain in "due season." (See Leviticus 26:4.) We are to discern His season and the kind of rain for which we should be interceding. (See Deuteronomy 11:14; 28:12.) God has a definite spiritual timetable for all His appointed seasons. Time itself has been ordered and designed by God. It is marked by a cycle of repetition, yet it flows from a beginning and toward a culmination. Prayer-intercession is vital to the understanding of times and seasons, vital to discerning God's purpose for that season. Time flows toward a divine purpose in a divinely appointed season. Individuals, congregations, or nations may find that through prayer-intercession they may intersect with appointed times, when God acts to keep history on its appointed course. God moves, creates circumstances, raises up leaders, deals with people as He seeks to fulfill appointed crossroads of history. Prayer-intercession allows us to discern God's dealings and God's time clock so that we may personally intersect with God's divinely appointed seasons.

What is this Season, this Appointed Time?

The two Greek words that are used for time are *chronos* and *kairos*. *Chronos* time designates a period or space of time. It is similar in meaning to the scientific way that westerners mark and speak of time. *Kairos* time characterizes the content and quality of the time. It is a moment made significant by a divine encounter with God.

Kairos is a due measure, proportion, a fixed or definite period or season; an opportune time. *Kairos* time is a time for prophecy to be fulfilled, a time suitable for a divine purpose to be accomplished. *Kairos* time speaks of a moment of opportunity marked by hearing God's voice, fresh and new. (See John 7:8; Romans 13:11; Psalm 119:126; Mark 1:15.)

"You will arise and have mercy on Zion; for the time to favor her, yes, the set time, has come" (Psalm 102:13).

Prayer-intercession moves the individual from the *chronos* place of living to the *kairos*; it moves him or her to a time to see promises fulfilled, a time for God to work powerfully.

We can discern, through prayer-intercession, which prayer areas to target, and then, with spiritual intensity, begin to intercede. Discerning the nature of the season allows us to pray with knowledge and faith. Scriptures point to different "set times" for which we may intercede.

It is time to break the bands of spiritual barrenness through prayer-intercession. "And Sarah shall bear to you at this set time next year" (Genesis 17:21).

This is a season of spiritual breakthrough that results in spiritual fruitfulness. We are to break all bands of limitations, restraints, resistance to hindrances, ungodly or self-made boundary lines.

It is time to receive spiritual blessings after sacrifices have been made through prayer-intercessors. "Then the Angel of the LORD called to Abraham a second time" (Genesis 22:15).

After the sacrifice of something sacred and precious, we should expect the blessings of the Lord. Our sacrifice may be time, money, personal convenience. If we sacrifice in order to fulfill our personal prayer-intercession time, we should expect supernatural blessings of the Lord to be released. Are you ready to make the sacrifices of your time, energy or lifestyle?

It is time to draw water from God's wells of refreshing through prayer-intercession. "And he made his camels kneel down outside the city by a well of water at evening time, the time when women go out to draw water" (Genesis 24:11). (See also Genesis 26:18; Isaiah 12:3; II Kings 3:19, 25; Numbers 21:16-17.)

The season of God upon us is a time of spiritual refreshing and revival. If we could visibly see the clock of God, it might be striking toward evening time. The last days are closing in around us. Another millennium is about to be launched. It is a time to draw water from God's available sources through intercessory prayer. To draw is my responsibility, depending on my hunger, my persistence. The water is God's part–His water is His refreshing power. The bucket we use to dip into God's well is faithful and persistent prayer-intercession.

It is time to resist satanic strategies through prayer-intercession. "But it happened about this time, when Joseph went into the house to do his work, and none of the men of the house was inside . . ." (Genesis 39:11).

Joseph had no idea of the situation he was walking into. He was totally innocent; he had no ill motive whatsoever. He had no idea that this was the time that the enemy of his life had chosen to ruin his future, to steal his destiny. In an instant, he was faced with life-changing choices. If Joseph yielded at this time to the satanic plot of adultery with his master's wife, he would forfeit his future as a deliverer and a trusted servant. Satan meant it for evil, as a time to destroy, but God turned a destructive time into a victorious time. Joseph demonstrated his integrity and trustworthiness.

Prayer-intercession prepares us for the unexpected moments of attack, the tests that come with no prior warning. It is time to build hedges through prayer for our souls, our churches, our families, our cities.

It is time to dream again through the power of prayer-intercession. "He slept and dreamed a second time" (Genesis 41:5).

In the atmosphere of prayer-intercession, dreams and visions surface more easily. There are sovereign times in our lives when God initiates dreams, gives us life-changing perspectives of our future. The word of the Lord came to Joseph a second time. After we have been tested, after we have been discouraged, after life seemingly has passed us by, then comes the second time. Then comes another chance. The word of the Lord came a second time to Jonah, to Peter, to John Mark. It is time to dream again, not only for ourselves, but also for our churches, our cities, our nation. Through intercessory prayer, faith and hope take on new powers, and our potential takes on new meaning.

It is time to confront our present, ungodly, degenerate culture through prayer-intercession. "Then the LORD appointed a set time, saying, 'Tomorrow the LORD will do this thing in the land' " (Exodus 9:5, 14, 18).

Our culture is one that has dethroned God and deifies man's achievements, exalting human reason above God's word. Our society trusts in education, science and medicine to solve all its problems. Our culture believes man is actually evolving into something better than what he now is.

Our culture today replaces absolute, moral standards with situational ethics and promotes illicit sexual pleasures and instant gratification. This is a culture adrift from God, and it will be judged accordingly if there is no repentance and returning to God. Through prayer-intercession, now is the time to pull down the strongholds that keep this culture captive. (See II Corinthians 10:3-4.) These strongholds can only be attacked through prayer. It is time to intercede and to stand in the gap for our day.

It is time to prepare another generation through the warfare of intercessory prayer. "At that time the LORD said to Joshua, 'Make flint knives for yourself, and circumcise the sons of Israel again the second time' " (Joshua 5:2).

Another generation is arising with different problems, needs, strengths, perspectives, a generation ready for a fresh encounter with the living God. Our enemy, the devil, will do all that is within His power to destroy this generation before it has a chance to fulfill God's purposes. This generation, which some call Generation X, has been targeted by the devil to remove it from God's reach. Note that abortion was legalized in

1973, bringing death to many in this generation. Forty-nine percent are from divorced homes, with the resultant lack, not only of fathers, but of security, hope and trust.

But through prayer-intercession, we can reach out and seize this generation. Every generation must receive a Christ visitation personally, must undergo a new circumcision of heart, a cutting away of the old. It is time to go to war, to go out and meet the enemy through prayer (II Samuel 11:1).

It is time to make bold requests through prayer-intercession. "For if you remain completely silent at this time, relief and deliverance will arise for the Jews from another place, but you and your father's house will perish. Yet who knows whether you have come to the kingdom for such a time as this?" (Esther 4:14).

Esther could not fully comprehend her time and season. The absolute miracle of her placement by God Himself was too far above her understanding. Could one young lady really make a historical difference, save a whole nation, turn the plot of the enemy into victory? How could this happen?

It did happen, and Esther's story has become one of the best known stories of the Bible. How many times and in how many ways have we heard this Scripture quoted to us: "Who knows whether you have come to the kingdom for such a time as this?"

It is time for us to realize that God has placed us in that family, that job, that marriage, that school, that church, that community, that state, that nation for such a time as this. Esther was on her knees, fasting and praying, before approaching the king with bold requests. "If I perish, I perish, but I will make this bold request."

In the 1800's, Philip Brooks, Pastor of the great Trinity Church of Boston, said, "Pray the largest prayers. You cannot think of a prayer so large that God in answering it will not wish you had made it larger. Pray not for crutches. Pray for wings!"

Our prayer must not be a vague appeal to His mercy or an indefinite cry for blessing, but the distinct request of definite need. It is time for us to enlarge our prayers. Jesus might want to ask us, as He did the blind man in Mark 10:51, "What do you want me to do for you?" Ask big. Ask bold. Now is the time. God is ready to hear and respond. Ask not for riches, honor or promotion for yourself, but ask for God's Kingdom to be extended, using your life and your resources today.

Bishop J.C. Ryle said, "Prayer has obtained things that seemed impossible and out of reach. It has won victories over fire, air, earth and water. Prayer opened the Red Sea. Prayer brought water from the rock and bread from heaven. Prayer made the sun stand still. Prayer brought fire from the sky on Elijah's sacrifice. Prayer overthrew the army of Sennacherib. Prayer has healed the sick. Prayer has raised the dead. Prayer has procured the conversion of countless souls."

God has poured out a spirit of grace upon the Church of the twenty-first century, a grace for fasting and prayer. Now is the time for all believers everywhere to take advantage of the canopy of grace for prayer-intercession. This season of intercession is a special, unique window that God has granted to us for global evangelism. The times and the seasons have been clearly defined for us now.

Lord, make us a house of intercession!

House of Prayer
In this house of prayer,
I come before you now,
Lifting my eyes to You,
Laying my burdens down.
And you will hear my prayer
As I'm calling out to You.
Touch me, Lord, in this house of prayer.

You have always been so faithful.
And I know your Word is ever true.
When I stand in need,
Your mercy reaches me.
Here I am, calling on Your name again;
Here I am, calling on Your name again.

Sharon Damazio, BT Music[2]

Further Study

1. What is the relationship between prayer-intercession and *kairos* time (John 7:8; Romans 13:11; Mark 1:25)?

2. Why is prayer-intercession important? What can prayer-intercession accomplish?

3. What are the "set times" you can intercede for in your own life, your family, your church, and your nation?

Notes

1. Charles Swindoll, <u>Growing Strong in the Seasons of Life</u>, 13.
2. Sharon Damazio, "House of Prayer" (Portland, Oregon: BT Music, 1997).

Chapter Two:
Serious Shifts in Our Nation's Culture

Mega-Shifts of Our Culture

The shifts that have taken place in our nation's culture are mega-shifts. Shifts in every major area of life, due to the impact of humanistic, syncretistic philosophies in our American culture, have eroded almost all godly, moral and spiritual value systems. We now live in a hostile culture, a culture separated from God, separated from God's Word, and separated from the reality of the Kingdom of God. How do we as Christians remain separated from this culture and keep from being engrafted into it, without becoming an isolated kind of people? How do we become sanctified without being weird in today's culture?

The word "culture" comes from the Latin word *colore*, which means "to till" or "to cultivate." It refers not only to tilling the soil, but also to the mind, the heart and the emotions. In the broadest sense, culture may be defined as the total pattern of human behavior and its products, as demonstrated in thought, speech, action and artifacts; and it is transmitted to succeeding generations through the tools, languages and systems of abstract thought.

Culture is not neutral.

Paul Sartre, philosopher (1905-1980), said, "Culture is not neutral. Life proceeds from the heart of man, and if the heart of man becomes wicked and perverted, so culture will be shaped by that wickedness and that perversion."[1]

II Timothy 3:1-10 gives us a description of the culture of the last days. Revelation 12-13 also describes the anti-Christ's system, which is a system that is anti-God and anti-everything that represents God. World culture will progress in evil until the whole earth will worship the beast, the false prophet, and there will be a great persecution against the true Church.

We are now living in a day in which culture has become a very powerful force to shape the minds and hearts of all people in it.

Discerning Our Cultural Stance

We do not want to be separated, weird and isolated, but neither do we want to be influenced by the world culture or the world mindset. We are Christians, and the Kingdom of God takes priority in our lives. We should only be responding to one lord, and that is the Lord Jesus Christ. We should only be responding to one absolute truth, and that is the Word of God.

> The culture in which we now live is rooted in atheism, agnosticism, humanism and new-age thinking, shaping people for a new kind of religion.

Yet, in our culture, there are many different influences and forces shaping the minds of the young and old alike. Using every avenue possible, our culture molds people into anti-God, anti-Church, anti-Christian and anti-Bible people. The culture in which we now live is rooted in atheism, agnosticism, humanism and new-age thinking, shaping people for a new kind of religion.

We need to understand the state to which the world has "evolved" to as we near the year 2000. The intellect has been replaced by self-will, and reason has been replaced by emotion. Morality has been replaced by relativism, and reality has been replaced by a social concept that is something made up by society itself, or whatever is politically correct.

We know that in John 17, the high-priestly prayer of the Lord Jesus Christ was that the Father would keep us, even as we are in the world, that He would watch over us, and that He would guard and preserve us in the midst of the perversity of any culture. Yet Scripture does say that He will not take us out of the world. Throughout the chapter, we see the phrases "keep them," "watch over," "not take out," but, "leave them in the world." We must understand that our responsibility as Christians is to live within our culture, yet not become like the culture.

All the ungodly, atheistic, agnostic, humanistic, and new-age seeds that are being sown in our culture, seeds sewn through the media, the educational system and the spirit of our day should not penetrate our hearts. We need to learn how to guard every aspect of our minds and spirits so as not to be shaped by the spirit of our day. When compared with previous generations of believers, we seem to be among the most thoroughly at peace with our culture, the least successful at transforming society and the most desperate for a meaningful faith.

This is the stark reality of what we face today as Christians living in the new world culture. Our

Let these ominous times press us to our knees...

motivation for gap standing intercession must be at an all time high, not a pessimistic "oh well" or an attitude of "this nation has gone to far." No! Let these ominous times press us to our knees and send us into the breach so that, with thousands of others, we turn the tide of history.

Three Main Elements That Shape Culture

- **The philosophic element** seeks intellectual answers to the basic questions of life. Philosophy is "a search for a general understanding of values and reality by chiefly speculative rather than observational means" (*Webster's New Collegiate Dictionary*, 1975 edition). The philosopher's beliefs, godly and ungodly, first shape the minds of the intellectual elite of a culture, who in turn influence the minds of college students and, ultimately, the minds of all the people in a given society.

- **The scientific element** seeks to understand the physical universe. The direction in which science moves is often set by the philosophic world-view of the scientist.

- **The religious element** includes all spiritual views which determine the choices and direction for individual lives and, ultimately, for all of society. Current religious views now accept all religions and all beliefs, whether new-age Eastern religions or atheist. Society is encouraged to accept these beliefs as a new way of thinking, even as a preferable way of thinking. All views are tolerated except those deemed narrow-minded (i.e., conservative fundamentalism).

These three elements shape our contemporary culture. As Christians, we believe that there are two main forces in the cosmos: the force of the devil, Satan himself, who is the father of lies and deception, and who operates with demonic help from the pit of hell; the force of the almighty God, the author of the truth, and who through the Word and the Spirit shapes the lives of people on this earth. Just as God can influence science, philosophy and religious elements, so can Satan. We know, of course, that He who is within us is greater than he who is in the world. That is, the Holy Spirit and the Word of God are more powerful than all the demons of hell.

But because the Word of God is not applied to every mind and every life, many people are not being shaped by the godly influence of the Holy Spirit or the Word of God. Therefore, the devil takes advantage of every opportunity to infiltrate with his deceptions and lies through any written material, music, videos, theater, or television—whatever source he invades is for the purpose of influencing every life and bringing it under his control.

We, as born-again believers, need to understand that the devil will not rest until we, too, are influenced by his lies. Therefore, we are encouraged in Scripture to put on the helmet of salvation, to guard our minds and to cast out all vain imaginations. This is not just a poetic thought for Christians; this is a survival tool in our twenty-first century culture. Intercessory prayers for our nation, with specific prayers regarding these shaping influences, are the Church's primary responsibility. If we fail, our very society can be destroyed.

Christianity is Becoming Acculturated

According to Webster's dictionary, the term "acculturated" is "the process of intercultural borrowing between diverse peoples, resulting in a new and blended pattern."

As our culture becomes increasingly removed from God, it in turn affects every member of society. Christianity is being acculturated, weakened by the culture we live in.

Everyone who lives within a specific culture has a world-view—a grid through which he or she sees the world. Our world-view includes our fundamental attitude about God, self, others and the basic way we look at life. Our world-view is not just about what we see, but about how we *interpret* what we see and experience. Our world-view determines how we think, how we choose to live our lives, our perception of what is truth.

World-view is often a complex network of ideas. Multiple perceptions and beliefs are interconnected and interwoven into a whole, moving us in a certain direction, so an individual's perception of truth, for example, can change periodically, every decade–or possibly every month. Our world-view shapes our values, controls our decisions. World-views cause shifts in culture. Some shifts have disastrous, catastrophic consequences for the people who adopt deceived world-views.

We need to perceive our world through a basic Christian world-view that honors God, honors the Bible, and honors godly values. Sadly, we all admit that there is an erosion of God-centered thought and Bible-based values in our culture.

Six Main Shifts of Culture

Our culture has made six main shifts we would call ungodly, areas that need to be addressed through a Christian mind-set and world-view. Though the shifts are easily recognized, they are not easily remedied.

The Shift of Science

Early scientists believed that the world was created by a wise and all-knowing God. Men like Newton were loyal to biblical teachings, as well as to science and discovery. Newton started from the premise that there was a personal God who had created the universe. He was a great student of Scripture, as well as one who studied the principles and laws of science. Pascal, a dedicated Christian, saw men as more than specks of dust lost in the universe. He believed that people were special, unique, because Christ died for them and their souls were eternal as the Bible taught, and he, therefore, merged scientific discoveries and biblical truths together.

The Christian view is that the world is worth scientifically searching into because God created it, but a shift in science occurred when belief in the Creator was questioned. The theory of evolution, published by Darwin in *Origin of the Species* in 1859 along with *Descent of Man* in 1871, posited a very different world-view and was ultimately embraced by scientists in other areas, such as psychology. Now man was a product of evolution, not of a true, living Creator. Man was only a step above an animal that responds to its basic needs with instincts, desires and passions, shaped and determined only by environment and chance. Man was now the center of an accidental creation, and this view caused a major shift in all other supporting philosophy, morality and theology.

The Shift of Philosophy

Philosophy and science are interrelated, affecting one another. When philosophy was influenced by a biblically based scientific view, with an absolute God and absolute principles, optimism and hope were possible. There was a true God who created this world for a purpose and created man with a purpose. Such optimism and hope is impossible to justify when there is no God and no meaning for existence.

Existentialism is one of the philosophical theories that has flourished in this century. It teaches autonomous freedom: reality is only what we perceive it to be, and we should live for the now because the future is not real. Only what is now is real. All things are merely the products of chance. All meaning is found only in experience.

Existentialism and relativism, that is, a lack of moral laws or moral absolutes, are still ruling philosophies. These ideas greatly influenced the decade of the 1960's. When the only reality was found in experience, not in God's word, the ultimate experience was drug induced. These philosophies opened up a whole new avenue that allowed Eastern religions to flood into our country. Religious experiences, such as Hinduism, Buddhism and other experience-based religions, flooded into America because our minds were wide open to them. Both drugs and Eastern religions seek truth inside one's own mind. Both negate reason. And both opened up a new hunger for the occult and the supernatural—which is a belief in an experience, not a belief in absolute truth.

The Shift of Theology

Soon even the theologians, especially the most liberal, began to doubt the Word of God. Carl Barth, one of the latest modern theologians, taught that the Bible contained many mistakes, but it could provide a religious experience. Thus began theology's marriage with existentialism: if there are no absolutes in the universe, there is no absolute Word of

God. It follows, then, that there is no real basis for applying biblical truth to morals or the law or history.

When belief in the supernatural is jettisoned, the way of explaining the devil and evil, heaven and hell, closes down. People are encouraged to run rampant, to choose a mere experience or to have any opinion or find whatever philosophy they would like to apply to their lives.

With this tremendous shift in science, philosophy and theology, even many of our religious institutions have embraced the theories of existentialism and relativism. Those schooled in relativism cannot accept the God of the Bible and Christ, as the only truth. We are left with religious words, without content and emotion.

The modern world-view and modern-day philosophies have no absolutes by which questions about life, eternal values, even morality itself, can be judged.

A Shift in Morality

A shift, from rules governing morality to situational ethics, from a moral to an immoral society, has occurred. In Frank Capra's autobiography of 1971, a film producer of our day writes:

> The winds of change blew through the dream factories. The hedonists, homosexuals, hemophiliacs, bleeding hearts, God-haters, quick-buck artists, who substituted shock for talent, all cried shake 'em, rattle 'em, because God is dead. Long live pleasure, nudity, wife-swapping, liberate the world from prudence, emancipate our films from morality.

We can see in the film industry, along with educational and political institutions, that a shift in morality has certainly taken place. What is morally right now is what the community says is right, not what the Bible says is right, not what God says is right, or what the church says is right, but whatever the community at large, the masses, now feel is right. Each person's own opinion is a standard for what is right and wrong. What is morally right to do is what is morally right for me.

The Greek philosopher Aristotle, born three centuries before Christ, simply says of morality, "Morality is found in moderation." It is not found in absolutes, not found in what would be biblically right or wrong, but simply in what one wants to do, as long as it is done in moderation. The hedonists simply say, "Right is what brings pleasure."

We have a whole society that is seeking experience, and pleasure, as long as individuals feel that it is in moderation. If it is not really hurting anyone else, it could not be wrong. Of course, many of the pleasures today are not just hurting people, but killing people. They are killing our marriages, killing our children, killing our educational systems. Now, largely due to immorality, viruses are killing millions of people. So we cannot really say, "Right is what brings me pleasure, as long as it does not hurt anyone." Our pleasures have now hurt many.

The *Nightline* moderator, Ted Koppel, was quoted in *Time Magazine*, June 27, 1987, as saying at the graduation ceremony at Duke University in Durham, North Carolina:

> We have actually convinced ourselves that slogans will save us. Shoot up if you must, but use a clean needle. Enjoy sex whenever and with whomever you wish, but wear a condom. No, the answer is no. Not because it isn't cool or smart or because you might end up in jail or dying in an AIDS ward. But no, because it's wrong, because we have spent five thousand years as a race of rational human beings trying to drag ourselves out of the primeval slime by searching for truth and moral absolutes. In its purest form, truth is not a polite tap on the shoulder; it is a howling reproach. What Moses brought down from Mt. Sinai were not the Ten Suggestions.[2]

The Shift of Absolutes

We have also had a shift from absolutes to relativism, a shift away from the rules of rationality to the acceptance of unconscious and motivational dynamics (i.e., a lack of absolutes) as the foundation of human behavior. This shift of absolutes to relativism or to humanism is something that we can see in every area of life. Secular humanism is a religion that dethrones God as the center of life and enshrines man instead. The aim of humanism and relativism is to replace theism–God–with man.

Frederick Moore Vinson, Chief Justice of the Supreme Court, 1946-1953, said, "Nothing is more certain in modern society than the principle that there are no absolutes. All is relative. All is experience. The only absolute allowed is the absolute insistence that there is no absolute."[3]

> **Nothing is more certain in modern society than the principle that there are no absolutes.**

We live in a strange, new world in which the relativity of Einstein is considered absolute and the absolutes of the Bible are considered relative.

An absolute is that which always applies, that which provides a final or ultimate standard. There must be an absolute if there are to be morals, and there must be an absolute if there are to be values. If there are no absolutes beyond man's opinions, then there is no final appeal to judge between individuals and groups whose moral judgements conflict. We are merely left with conflicting opinions. We need absolutes if our existence is to have meaning! If we are to have a theory of knowing, how do we know we know, how can we be sure that what we think we know of the world outside ourselves really corresponds with what is there? The only way to really do that is to have an absolute basis from which to work. Francis Shaeffer so aptly described the crises of our day when he said, "Modern man has both feet firmly planted in mid-air."[4]

As Christians, we need to maintain our belief in absolutes with conviction. Biblical convictions never change but bring honor to God. Our convictions and absolutes must be seen in our daily living, and we must be consistent with them.

The Shift from Monotheism

The shift from monotheism to polytheism is so evident in our culture today that it is absolutely frightening. It does not take much research to understand that pluralism is fashionable and belief in the one God of the Bible is not. As Christians we need to establish and defend the firm foundation by which we live our Christian lives, in order to pass on the godly heritage of our Christianity to the next generation, which is surrounded by relativism and polytheism. Martin Luther, in dealing with his day and culture, said:

He who would live soberly, righteously and godly must take up the Cross. He must not allow himself to be misled, even though he has to live alone, like Lot in Sodom and Abraham in Canaan, among none but the glutinous, the drunken, the incontinent, the unrighteous, false and ungodly people. His environment is world and must remain world. He has to resist and overcome the enticements of earth, censoring worldly desires. To live right in this present world, mark you, is like living soberly in a saloon, chastely in a brothel, godly in a gaiety hall, uprightly in a den of murderers. The character of the world is such as to render our earthly life difficult and distressing until we longingly cry out for death and the day of judgement and await them with ardent desire.[5]

The Results of These Shifts

The immorality of our society is evident everywhere–pornography, prostitution, easy divorce, easy abortion, unwed mothers, fornication, homosexuality, nude or topless bars, gay bars, X-rated television, X-rated videos, MTV, particular cable shows. The moral filth and seduction that floods into the homes of millions of people by all the different media avenues constantly causes even more devaluing of the human soul and of our morality.

We live in a culture in which moral laws are vanishing. God-given moral laws are not recognized or sought after. Immorality is glorified in our literature and songs. Society does not believe in timeless, moral laws, and it does not believe in laws against laws. The *Humanist Manifesto* speaks for itself, quoted here:

> In the area of sexuality, we believe that intolerant attitudes are often cultivated by orthodox religions which unduly repress sexual conduct. The right to birth control, abortion and divorce should be recognized. While we do not approve of exploitive, denigrating forms of sexual expression, neither do we wish to prohibit, by law or social sanction, sexual behavior between consenting adults.[6]

The humanists have put forth their goals and their intents for our culture. Our culture has been responding in every way to these new shifts as if eager for every ungodly seed to be planted deep into the soil of the heart and mind of our culture, which then brings forth even more perversion and brokenness. Our hope is in the revival of prayer. Our hope is a return to our primary focus of individuals and churches that intercede.

Further Study

1. What are some of the main elements that help to shape a culture?

2. Describe some of the main shifts that our culture has made in the past few years? Which of these shifts do you think have most influenced Christian churches in America?

3. Why do you think it is important to understand our culture? How can we understand our culture without becoming involved in its destructive aspects?

Notes

1. Paul Satre.

2. Ted Koppel, Time Magazine (June 27, 1987).

3. Fredrick Moore Vinson.

4. Francis Schaeffer, How Shall We Then Live (Grand Rapids, MI: Fleming-Revell, 1976).

5. Martin Luther.

6. Paul Kurtz, ed., Humanist Manifesto (Prometheus Books, 1973), 18.

Chapter Three:
Increasing Cultural Tensions

World and National Tensions

Our world and national culture have many tensions that must be handled by wise Christians who believe in the absolute truth of the Word of God and the power of the Holy Spirit to keep them on the right path and to give them wisdom to discern how to live in this culture. These tensions must be faced with the power of the Holy Spirit, the living Word of God and power-filled intercessory prayer.

Moral Tensions

In America alone, statistics show that there are 1,871 women raped every day. We live in a sexually confused world, where 56 million now have sexually transmitted diseases–that is one in every five people in America. Moral tension, when it comes to sexuality, is real. The young are under particularly great pressure in our day, resulting in many more teenage abortions, many more unwed teen parents. We live in a society that says, "Get sex, get all you can, and do not feel bad about it. Get rid of your guilt any way you can because that is the old Judeo-Christianity guilt-trip they try and put on you. There is nothing wrong with having sex." The whole world is shouting it out, and we, as Christians, feel like a minority that is holding out.

God honors virginity. Being sexually pure in marriage, the Bible teaches, is the way to have a happy marriage. Yes, we do have moral tensions. But we believe in the absolutes of the Word of God and take the

Word of God as our guide in the area of morality. With these absolutes we will not fall into the trap of deception and damage by a morally corrupt world.

Lifestyle Tension

We have lifestyle tensions because of the temptations of materialism, of getting everything we can because we think that possessions bring happiness and fulfillment.

Value System Tension

Theologian Carl Henry, in his book, *Twilight of a Great Civilization*, summarizes the tension between those who become prisoners of modern times and those who have freed themselves, who will likely be seen by future generations as men and women of character and virtue.[1] Immortality belongs to those who seek to apply the principles of the Bible to all the complications of modern life, who preserve a devout and virtuous family life, who are faithful to the godly values of yesterday, today and tomorrow.

Media Tension

In the last generation, television has changed drastically, and is now actively promoting evil, promoting sex and sensuality, promoting homosexuality and promoting hatred toward God and the Church. Family shows are not suitable for the family anymore. Unless the programs are made for the Simpsons and the Adams family, how can anyone really receive anything from television in its current state?

"One way to help your soul, intellect and moral order, at least for the individual, is to turn off the television" (Cal Thomas).[2] Many advocate tolerating no television, some advocate discipline over the television. Whatever way you choose, you must understand that what is put into the young mind will soon be put into the young belief system. Therefore, discipline over what is viewed on television is certainly worthy of exhortation.

Music Tension

In *The Closing of the American Mind*, Alan Bloom said:

Nothing is more singular about this generation than its addiction to music. This is the age of music and the states of soul that accompany it.

Today a very large population proportion of young people between the ages of ten and fifteen live for music. It is their passion. Nothing else excites them as it does. They cannot take seriously anything alien to music. Nothing that surrounds them, school, family or church, has anything to do with their musical world. At best, that ordinary life is neutral, but mostly it is an impediment drained of vital content, even a thing to be rebelled against. But rock music has one appeal: young people know that rock has the beat of sexual intercourse.[3]

That we are living in a new age of music was clear as Bill Clinton took over the White House as President of the United States. *Fleetwood Mac* sang "Can't Stop Thinking About Tomorrow," which became the anthem of the 1992 Presidential Campaign for Bill Clinton, *Jefferson Airplane* played at the Democratic Convention, and *Peter, Paul and Mary* sang at the Inaugural Gala. This music played a prominent part in the lives of the Baby Boomers who have now become the nation's leaders and who now choose such styles of music to represent America.

"The world-view of modern man shapes modern music. Man is isolated and helpless in the grip of forces he does not understand. He has fallen prey to inner conflict, tension, anxiety, and fear" (Frances Shaeffer).[4]

When we consider that music is the expression of man's heart, the expression of man's values and core belief systems, we can understand why music is so discordant, its stars so perverted, today. There are many different types of popular music today, but one thing goes without question: any music that elevates homosexuality, rape, sexual intercourse before marriage, adultery and a lack of respect for either gender is a music that should not be listened to by anyone, especially a believer. We can understand that the wickedness of the human heart, taken captive by the devil, would enjoy music that exalts sin in every way. But the believer's heart, which has been redeemed by Christ and washed by the blood of Jesus, should not find pleasure in listening to music that promotes rebellion, perversion, homosexuality and adultery.

We are constantly barraged by ever-increasingly violent new styles of music. Music that promotes murder, a music that promotes hatred for anything that is godly, is not music that should be heard. Satan understands the power of music. If parents are afraid to shape, form and train their children, they need to know that there is a multi-billion dollar entertainment industry out there that will gladly to do it for them. One of the great multi-billion dollar industries in the television industry is MTV (Music Television), which plays music 24 hours a day, and most of that music needs to be brought under great scrutiny through the absolutes of the Word of God. We need to resist Satan's snare in music.

Satan has always had a purpose for music and has always wanted to use music to shape the minds of people. Satan has always wanted to use music to move man's mind, will and emotions away from God, to penetrate his soul and move man into rebellion, immorality and perversion. Satan has always wanted to use music to break down man's moral conscience, to continually lift a perverted standard as cool, the "in" thing. The tales in music of rape, violence, hatred, rebellion and sex are the main ingredients of modern alternative, pop, rap, rock and even country music. Satan has always wanted to encourage people to worship themselves, worship idols of music and musicians, until music has become a religion in itself.

Addiction to music that causes inner problems of attitude and morality is an addiction that a person needs to be rid of. If you would look up in an encyclopedia the characteristics of addiction, as stated concerning a person that is addicted to food, drugs or alcohol, you would find these statements, which can then be applied to music:

- The tendency of an addict to deny his addiction.
- A sacrifice of relationships for the addiction.
- A compulsion to engage in the addiction at any time.
- A practice of secrecy until others accept it.
- The creation of an appetite that is never satisfied.
- Unusual efforts to feed the addiction.
- Using any money necessary for the addiction.
- A readiness to defend the cause of the addiction.
- A need to involve others in the addiction.
- A reaction to those who disagree with the addiction.

We must, by the absoluteness of the Word of God, discern destructive music. Does it promote rebellion in any form? Does it promote the world's view? We need to make what I call "an Acts 15:20 commitment." This is a commitment to resist any music that promotes idolatry in any form, especially the idols of rock music and rock stars. It is a commitment to resist any music that promotes sexual immorality, anything that stirs up sensuality or lasciviousness. A commitment to resist any music that strangles the Christ-life in me or the Christ-life in others. If it stran-gles—that is, causes indifference to the Word of God—get rid of it! If it causes coldness toward prayer or worship, put it aside! If it causes an atti-tude or reaction toward any authority, its roots are in the pit of hell. If it causes any slipping in my moral standard, this is a satanic plot to destroy me. If it causes my flesh to desire worldly things or carnal things, this music is not rooted in the Bible, in Christ, or in the Holy Spirit.

Make a commitment to resist any music that moves us away from the power and simplicity of the blood of Jesus, His work and His sacrifice.

Gap standing Prayer for Cultural Tensions

Now is the time for "standing in the gap" prayer. Now is the time to repent with humility and ask God to heal our land. The darker the hour is, the brighter the light will be. Will you move into the gap with inten-tional intercession for a nation that has turned away from God?

The cry of our nation's heart to the church is: please, intercede for us.

If we could hear the cry of our nation, it would sound something like what Pharaoh said to Moses. "And Pharaoh said, 'I will let you go, that you may sacrifice to the Lord your God in the wilderness; only you shall not go very far away. Intercede for me' " (Exodus 8:28).

The cry of our nation's heart to the church is this: "Do not go very far away. Do not separate yourselves from us too far. Church, please, intercede for us. Someone, please stand in the gap for us. We are lost, blind, without hope. We are the sick, the confused. We have lost our way. Intercede for us! Do not go too far away!" Our call is to stand in the gap with compassionate intercession for our nation.

Charles Finney, the evangelist who was used mightily in revivals, spoke of the crucial importance of prayer in interceding for revival in a nation. In 1830 he said, "Prayer is the indispensable condition of pro-moting revival. Unless I had the experience of prayer I could do noth-ing. If for even a day or an hour I lost the spirit of grace and supplication, I found myself unable to preach with power and efficiency or to win souls by personal conversation."[5]

Our Prayer as Gap Standing Intercessors

"Oh God, we bend our knees and in humility bow before You. You have rejected us. Your judgment upon our nation is deserved. We have sinned. You have broken us with Your righteous anger. You have shaken this nation to its foundation. We are desperate and we are in Your hands. Have mercy, oh God! Send a spirit of repentance upon our land. We are now reaping what we have sown for generations. Our families are being destroyed, our young are being murdered, our youth are under various deceptions, other gods are worshipped, our cities crumble with crime, violence and perversion. Our only hope is Your undeserved mercy. Hear the cry of the millions who pray! Hear the cry of those who stand in the gap for this dying nation. Heal our land. Send revival, we pray! Accept our repentance. Please let Isaiah 44:3-5 be now our portion."

"For I will pour water on him who is thirsty, and floods on the dry ground; I will pour My Spirit on your descendants, and My blessing on your offspring; they will spring up among the grass like willows by the watercourses" (Isaiah 44:3-4).

Further Study

1. Apart from prayer, what strategies do Christians often employ to deal with the tensions in our society? Do you think these are effective? Why or why not?

2. Draw up a list of specific messages our culture sends us concerning values, lifestyle, and morality? Are these messages consistent with Biblical teaching? Why or why not?

3. Do you believe that our culture is beyond hope? What can Christians do that is most needed for our culture today?

Notes

1.   Carl F. Henry, <u>Twilight of a Great Civilization</u> (Wheaton, IL: Crossway Books, 1998).

2.   Cal Thomas, <u>Cal Thomas Report</u>.

3.   Alan Bloom, <u>The Closing of the American Mind</u> (Touchstone Books, Simon & Schuster, 1987), 68, 73.

4.   Francis Schaeffer, <u>How Shall We Then Live</u> (Grand Rapids, MI: Fleming-Revell, 1976), 193.

5.   Charles Finney, <u>Lectures on Revival</u>.

Chapter Four:
Shattering Experiences Destroying a Generation

A herd of musk oxen was under attack by a pack of arctic wolves. The wolves were after the young of the herd. As the wolves approached their quarry, the adult musk oxen bunched into an unbroken circle with the young in the center. The oxen's deadly rear hooves were as effective as a barricade against the wolves. As long as they remained in this position of unified resistance, the wolves were held at bay. Then a single ox broke out of the herd, causing the rest to scatter into small groups of two or three. Once scattered, every young calf fell victim to the onslaught of the wolves. Thus, even in nature, we see the importance of corporate unity in warfare.

Gap standing intercession has awesome potential to change the course of lives, cities, nations and world culture. We see the power of gap standing intercessors as we study the lives of Abraham, Moses, David, Esther and, of course, Jesus. The Church is called to be one Body joined together by many members. When we appear before the Lord to stand in the gap, we do so as one man, with one heart and one voice in one accord. The demons of hell and the powers of darkness that war against our nation fear the force of an interceding church.

We have spoken of gap standing intercession for a nation. Now let us understand gap standing intercession for a generation: the intercession of God's people for the young generation, currently called by some "Generation X," which could become, through intercessory prayer, "Generation Destiny."

Understanding Generation X

For intercession to be made as effectively and powerfully as possible, we will examine this generation and strive to understand its roots, what shapes its attitudes and values, emotional and spiritual needs. Although we will specifically deal with Generation X, these generational disorders and characteristics apply to any generation.

> ...the Church is responsible to minister to each generation the eternal truth of the Gospel of Jesus Christ

Each generation must have its own spiritual encounter with God. Each generation can be characterized by certain traits and personality patterns its members share in common, defining characteristics due to cultural trends and spiritual states. Still, the Church is responsible to minister to each generation the eternal truth of the gospel of Jesus Christ.

"One generation passes away and another generation comes, but the earth abides forever" (Ecclesiastics 1:4).

Every generation is marked by perversions of the reigning culture and is shaped by influences from the scientific and philosophical community. When spiritual powers move through the Church of Jesus Christ and through the believers in every country of the world, every culture is affected by the Kingdom of God. When there is a lack of Holy Spirit power and Holy Spirit initiative within the Church to reach out and touch the world, then the result is that the world changes the Church. The Church was never meant to be a fortress in which we would stay and guard all the truths and the precious, sacred things that God has imparted unto us so that the world would not spoil or ruin them. Rather, we have been given a commission to go out into the world and be salt and light. We have been given a commission to go out and preach the gospel to every creature, in every culture. Each and every generation must know the impact of the gospel of the Lord Jesus Christ.

Throughout history, some generations have been touched by a revival spirit, have experienced a great move of the Kingdom of God that changes that culture and that entire generation. These generations are blessed by the powerful moving of the Holy Spirit, while other generations live their whole lives in the midst of a spiritual desert and spiritual confusion. Exodus 1 says that when the children of Israel were in the land of Egypt, they cried out, and the Lord heard them. They cried out because of their captivity and their misery, and out of that cry came the response of an Almighty God, who delivered them from Egypt and took them into a new land.

Every generation must cry unto the Lord. As we have seen, the culture, with all its different influences, has a great, invisible and shaping hand upon every generation. We now face the new generation nearing adulthood. It could truly be said that this is a generation that knows not the Lord, as in Judges 2:10. Every time a generation arises out of a spiritual vacuum, it is a generation that will not know the Lord.

Generation X is so called because it seems to be the invisible generation, without notable, easily defined, dominant characteristics. Those born between 1965 and 1980, who are the post-Baby Boomers, are called the Re-Generation: this generation lacks its own identity and creates one by reviving, repeating, or just ripping off the past. It is a generation that has been told, 'You lack purpose and cause.' This generation has been accused of being lazy, dysfunctional and anti-intellectual, and this certainly seems accurate in many cases.

Generation X-ers are obviously frustrated from reading all the material written about their own generation, criticizing their laziness and their dysfunctional behavior. *Time Magazine* estimated that there are about 48 million people between the ages of eighteen and twenty-nine years of age, within the X Generation, and stated that these are lost, not even searching souls; they are empty-headed, and most of them torn by divorce. Generation X has a variety of descriptions. Many have tried to define this quickly-maturing generation that desperately needs to be touched by the gospel of Jesus Christ.

This generation has been called the "motor-booty generation," "boomerang generation," "repair generation," "disillusioned generation," "invisible generation" and "searching generation." Those in this age group have been nicknamed "slackers," "twenty-somethings," "grunge kids," "thirteeners," "busters," "tweeners," "late bloomers," "post-bloomers," "boomlets." These are terms from those who, from a secular standpoint, are trying to understand and define this generation.

I would like to define this generation from a spiritual standpoint, so we may discern the causes of the problems in this generation and the subsequent remedies.

Discerning the Spiritual Pulse of this Generation

This generation could be characterized as a people who have no god to serve. Generation X-ers do not understand the God of the Bible, and they do not trust the Church. They believe that religious people are weird and morality is a moment-by-moment choice. People with biblical convictions are dangerous. To be cool, they must lack purpose and passion, have nothing to live for and nothing to die for. The dominant characteristics of Generation X are also the same characteristics possessed by much of the world. Generation X-ers have been shaped by a series of unique experiences they have encountered, some by choice, some without choice.

Experiences Shared First in Generation X

This is the first generation to be raised, not only in the television culture, but by television. The television has been their electronic baby-sitter; it has been called the "glass nipple." By age eighteen, Generation X-ers have spent six of their years watching television.

This is the first generation to be educated by MTV. MTV produces new mindsets, espouses new values outside any moral or philosophical boundaries. MTV sets the agenda for lifestyle choices and is a primary source of information and influence, across all ethnic and religious backgrounds. MTV develops its own culture and politics for a generation.

This is the first generation to have a three-minute attention span. It has been noted that this generation cannot seem to focus on one thing. Generation X-ers have fragmented thinking. Bombarded with media technology, it is hard for them to focus on the realities of everyday life. Their attention span is very short, and they need to be jolted with entertainment. This causes problems in concentration not only for education, but also for relationships and for work itself. Many churches are scrambling to try many different programs, hoping to capture the minds of this new generation. They do not have a sufficiently long-term attention span for church services that last longer than ninety minutes, sixty minutes or even thirty minutes. Messages have been cut down to twenty minutes, some as brief as fifteen minutes, trying to capture this generation of young people, only to find that they have become restless and bored and have drifted off, despite all the different techniques to interest them.

This is the first generation to have little or no hope for a better future. This generation is pessimistic, even visionless. Generation X-ers do not plan for the long haul because they do not see the long haul as a reality worth planning for. This generation sees the world blowing up at any moment. Terrorism is on the rise; new plagues appear continually. Millions are dying from AIDS and other similar sexually transmitted diseases. This generation does not have great hope for a long future or a better future. The environmentalists have painted a terrifying picture of our dying planet, of the disintegration of our world. We continually hear horror stories of all the different species that are becoming extinct. We hear of the hideous abuse of our earth, the suffering because of man's greed and ignorance of nature.

So what does this generation have to look forward to? A disease-ridden society vainly trying to protect a world teetering on the edge of extinction?

This is the first generation to have access to global information. Generation X-ers, just by the push of a button, can turn on the television, can watch a videocassette—can instantly plug into bombarding news of global problems, population growth problems, environmental breakdowns, global wars, famines, earthquakes and continual national upheaval. They can read of assassinations and uprisings. They can watch wars on television. They can track almost anything going on in the world through the global network communication system. This is information overload, and it cannot be handled by anyone. The overwhelming information is not just mind-boggling for Generation X, but for any generation.

This is the first generation to have little or no trust in authority—civil, parental, religious or divine. Having seen so many violations by authority figures, trusting authority requires a quantum leap for this generation. Generation X-ers have watched presidents lie; they have read about Watergate and have experienced subsequent presidents who have had different kinds of Watergate-like scandals. They have watched some church leaders fall—through serious immorality, lying, fraud and plainly ripping off people. Through the media, they have watched countless people in authority who have violated all moral laws. This generation has concluded that authority is not to be trusted.

For the Church, this obviously creates an immense problem since we claim that God is our authority and the Bible–as well as those who preach and teach the Bible–should be trusted. Those who bring the gospel to this generation ought to be trusted. But those in the Church who have violated the moral laws of the Word of God have harmed the gospel message. Other secular leaders have violated the moral trust of this society. All this has contributed to deep feelings of mistrust, suspecting "hidden agendas" from all those in positions of authority.

This is the first generation to embrace a polytheistic religious worldview. In this culture there are many alternative gods–gods that can be studied in history, Eastern gods, or gods formed from personal beliefs–or individuals might even become their own gods! Culture is becoming increasingly hostile to those who are not tolerant of other religious beliefs–especially, the Church. The Church is the one institution that cannot be tolerant of beliefs that do not lift up Jesus Christ, or the belief that the Bible is not the ultimate truth to which every man should bow, mind, heart and soul.

The movement underway in America which blends many beliefs together, creating an amalgamation of whatever beliefs anyone might want to espouse, is gathering such force that it will ultimately become the means to persecute the Church of Jesus Christ. In America and many parts of Europe, this is the first generation to embrace a polytheistic religious world-view in our educational systems. Christianity is not taught as a religion in the schools; it is resisted. Now students can study other kinds of belief systems and religions, but the one that birthed this country and has been a blessing to many countries is not even allowed to be mentioned in our educational systems.

This is the first generation to live in a culture in which relativism–that is, a lack of moral laws and moral absolutes–has become the ruling philosophy. Relativism affects every decision and every belief, morally and socially, in our culture. Evidence of the sweeping impact of relativism has become obvious in all new educational materials used in our schools and universities. Anyone who believes in a standard of moral laws, moral absolutes–especially any of the moral laws expressed in Scripture–is considered narrow-minded, bigoted and stupid.

This is the first generation to witness the demise of true biblical Christianity. Many churches in America and throughout the world–we are speaking now of thousands–have become religious institutions without the true power of the Holy Spirit because of their loss of core Christian truths. They do not believe that Jesus was born of a virgin, they do not believe in the inerrancy of Scripture, they do not believe in a bodily second coming of the Lord Jesus Christ to this earth, and they do not believe in the centrality of the message of the Cross, which preaches a true repentance, to believe and to be water baptized, nor do they think that these should be added to church doctrine. Biblical thinking produces biblical convictions–and we are faced with the absence of that now in Christianity. Many churches have no real evidence that their members are born-again, according to even the most basic level of biblical understanding.

A new, casual approach to things sacred accompanies a devastating ignorance of the Scriptures throughout much of Christianity. Again, as Generation X-ers rise to maturity, they begin to understand that these religious institutions do not have Christian substance, that these religious institutions do not have any more to offer than an Eastern religion or a new age mind religion. Although they do, at times, accept invitations to visit certain religious institutions and Christian Protestant institutions, they are left empty and questioning, wondering if this kind of religion could really deceive so many people into believing that it is the chief religion of the world.

Consequently, we see those who have been searching for answers, but have been influenced by the philosophy and world mindset of relativism. When they encounter this pseudo form of Christianity, they are not asked to believe nor are they brought to conviction. They are brought only to a cynical attitude. As a result, we now face a generation that needs to hear the true gospel of the Lord Jesus Christ preached by Scripture with the power of the Holy Spirit, or we have no chance of turning Generation X toward the Church and true Christianity. All of Christianity is being reviled because of these religious institutions that are vacant of any substance or reality of God.

This is the first generation that does not know a strong, stable, traditional family lifestyle. Members of this generation have been called "latchkey kids," with career or divorced parents. Television programs such as *90210* or *Real World* (the MTV family) depict happy kids in their new nontraditional families. The traditional family is seen as something from the past that is quickly fading out, shortly to be replaced with a new American and a new-world family. Our culture preaches that it is possible to achieve the intimacy of marriage by living together without being married, without having the responsibility of any covenant commitment.

This is the first generation to be overwhelmed with fantasy thinking and living. The game industry has produced an "unreal" generation through video games. Now comes one of the newest techniques, called "virtual reality." This is a technology that allows users to experience first-hand the sights, sounds and textures of worlds created entirely by computers, turning fantasy into reality fantasy. Unfortunately, people will choose to live in fantasy, thinking that it is reality, instead of choosing the reality of Christ, because they think *Christ* is fantasy. Generation X-ers will be so fantasized out of their minds and their imaginations that to preach to them a real gospel or a real Bible will prove impossible for them to grasp. They will not comprehend what it means to live the Christian life in the real world. They would rather opt for a fantasy religion or a mind religion that will take them out of this planet and out of this boring lifestyle into something more exciting and more "real," a world of make-believe.

This is the first generation to face a multitude of new mystery plagues. AIDS has only been in existence a comparatively short time, yet thousands, and even millions, of people have contracted this disease and are dying from it. Estimates are that several million people will die in the next five years before more effective ways of treating this vicious disease are discovered. Numerous other diseases–dozens of kinds of cancer, heart disease, viral infections–are taking thousands of lives every year in our world.

This generation is faced with mystery plagues with no proven cures, and no ways of escape. It seems unfair that a mother of six would be killed by the AIDS virus because of a tainted blood transfusion. Because of such mistakes, we are daily reminded of the fragility of life today. To this generation, living seems fraught with danger. Generation X-ers expect these diseases and these mystery plagues to possibly take their lives someday. There is a great deal of fear, anxiety and hopelessness that rapes the hearts and souls of this generation. When we preach the gospel and the God of the Bible, we will be questioned as to why God would allow these kinds of mysterious plagues to take the lives of innocent children, innocent young people and innocent adults.

This is the first generation to become totally computerized and modernized with new inventions every day. We can now send the *Encyclopedia Britannica* across the Atlantic Ocean, electronically, six times a minute. If the technology of the automobile industry could keep up with computer technological advances, a Rolls Royce would get three million miles to the gallon, cost less than three dollars, and would fit on the head of a pin. We are seeing such a mega-leap into the future with computer technology that even people on the cutting edge of this industry are astounded. This generation knows computers. Generation X-ers can do their shopping, their letter writing and their homework all from computers. Many of them will one day run their businesses from their home computers.

But computers have changed life. There is less personal interaction when a person can do everything and get everything needed by working at a computer. This again will create a great challenge for the Church, for the Kingdom of God, to make inroads into this generation when it is so closed off from social life and from corporate gatherings as we see in the Church today. A generation obsessed with fantasy, cruising the worldwide web and virtual reality will not look to the Church for its information. The Church is usually twenty years behind whatever is the scientific, cutting-edge technology of the day.

This is the first generation to experience what historians call "break points." After long periods of stability or status quo comes a burst of energy, a burst of explosive mega-changes. The individual or society never returns to the original starting place again. Many of those writing about break points believe that this is a generation of break points in which there will be many bursts of explosive changes that will stretch and test the minds and hearts from the youngest to the oldest. This generation has seen some of that happen with countries changing so quickly, and with the computer changing industry and the workplace.

Sometimes within only a year or two, careers and jobs that people have studied for and prepared for no longer exist. These are called "break point decades" or "break point years."

For this generation, anything less than unrelenting, constant change seems boring and unreal.

This generation is being raised in a break point atmosphere and environment. We who are 35, 45, 55, 65 and 75 were not raised in a generation of break points. We who only saw break points every ten, fifteen, or twenty years are now seeing them every year or every six months. For this generation, anything less than unrelenting, constant change seems boring and unreal.

Again, the Church is challenged. What do we have to offer this generation? Do we offer them a boring, predictable church service with a boring, predictable church message that is irrelevant to their lives and their thinking, yet expect that Generation X-ers will flood into the House of God and take our form of Christianity and adapt it to their lifestyles? I think not! I think we are facing our own mega-changes and our own break points. The Church, at this time in history, needs to break through the spirit world into the Kingdom of God, bring forth the treasures of that Kingdom and present them to this generation. To do that, we need the power of the Holy Spirit to once again move in the hearts of people in such a way that Christianity becomes a religion of reality, substance and power—a call to a life of adventure, not boredom.

Gap Standing Remedies for this Generation

The only way the Church will become effective is to once again see the miracle-working power of Jesus heal the sick, open the blind eyes, make the cripple walk, heal those with AIDS and see deliverance take place. God is a prayer-answering God, and the

I am advocating the life of Jesus kind of a Church.

Church should be known as a place where things happen. If the Church is not a place where things happen, this generation will look beyond it for other exciting experiences and institutions. I am not advocating some kind of a super-hyped Church, but I am advocating a book of Acts Church. I am advocating the life of Jesus kind of a Church. I am advocating a Church so filled with the power of God that when people come into it, they feel the same power as those who came into earthly contact with Jesus. I am advocating that when the gospel is preached, something happens to sinners, their minds are stunned, conviction comes to their spirits and they cry out, "What must we do to be saved? !"

A Church that has diluted the gospel into some kind of social message or entertainment center will miss this generation. This generation is being entertained to death. Generation X-ers do not need more entertainment; they need truth! And truth is found in the Scriptures, preached with the anointing and the power of the Holy Spirit. Our Church does not need all kinds of user-friendly ideas, ways and means to seize the minds of this generation. If we try to become so smart in man's ways, we will miss the simple remedy to reach this generation. Every generation responds to the gospel of Jesus preached by the power of the Holy Spirit. Let us not stray off course, pursuing all kinds of methods to present our message to try to reach a confused and hurting generation. The gospel is enough for any generation, and Jesus Christ is the same yesterday, today and forever.

Although many characteristics of Generations-X could be viewed as hopeless, one thing is certain; this generation can be reached by the gospel and shall be reached by the gospel, especially the gospel preached by the power of the Holy Spirit!

Further Study

1. What are some of the characteristics of Generation X?

2. What experiences have shaped Generation X? How do you think these experiences have shaped this generation's view of God? Of Christianity?

3. How can the spiritual condition of Generation X or any generation be remedied?

Chapter Five:
Gripping Bondages of Our Nation

This generation has developed several "bondages" due to cultural and philosophical influences that, coupled with satanic strategies of the evil one, have brought ruin. Modern psychology has married liberal theology, only to produce a philosophy that has redefined God, sin, man and man's problems. We do not need to look to modern psychology or liberal theology to find answers for this generation. We need to understand the bondages of this generation and then apply the simple Word of God to each one of them, believing that the Holy Spirit will ignite the truth and save this generation.

There are several bondages which can be discerned and which affect all within this generation.

The Cynicism Bondage

"Nothing is worth believing or respecting; everything is worth criticizing and jesting about."

"And it shall come to pass at that time that I will search Jerusalem with lamps, and punish the men who are settled in complacency, who say in their heart, 'The Lord will not do good, nor will He do evil' " (Zephaniah 1:12).

Cynicism can be heard in the confession of one Generation X-er, "By age thirty we will have moved on to more mature experiences like infidelity, starting our own ad agencies, breast cancer, or getting run over while riding a bicycle."

This is cynicism. This is a bondage that comes to a culture removed from all truth and reality about living, without the hope which comes through the power of the Holy Spirit and the Word of God. When a culture no longer has any hope in God or the Bible and has torn loose from all of its spiritual moorings, cynicism is the bondage that creeps into every soul and heart. Each generation needs to understand that there is a God in heaven, that God has given us His Word and that the Bible is trustworthy.

God honors certain principles and acknowledges people for their confession of faith and their ability to respond to His Spirit. Faith and belief, though seemingly hard at times, are the only way we can accept the ways of God. We cannot understand everything God does, but we must believe that God is good and just and that the Bible explains His character in such a way that we can trust Him.

We must not give in to cynicism, we must not develop the speech of a cynical tongue, we must not develop an unbelieving, cynical mind. And we must not lose all hope and faith for the future. We resist this cynicism bondage.

The Fatalism Bondage

"Nothing really matters. Nothing works out when you believe or even when you do all the right things."

"And He said: 'I will hide My face from them, I will see what their end will be, for they are a perverse generation, children in whom is no faith' " (Deuteronomy 32:20).

A fatalistic mindset is one that will surrender to vain imaginations and hopelessness of the heart, unable to believe in destiny or finding the will of God for one's life. "No one can find fulfillment in life. Even if you do all the right things, it will not work out because life has its strange twists and turns" (see Ecclesiastics 3:17). And so fatalism sets in. We believe that there is a cure for the bondage of fatalism.

"To everything there is a season, a time for every purpose under heaven" (Ecclesiastics 3:1).

We, as believers in Jesus Christ, resist this spirit of fatalism because we believe that God works everything out according to the counsel of His own will and there is a season for every purpose under heaven; as God works in and through my life, I tap into His purposes, and I begin to understand what God wants in me and through me. I am not a speck of dust being blown in any direction by the wind of life. I am controlled by a living God. I am under the hand of a living God.

"And we know that all things work together for good to those who love God, to those who are called according to His purpose. For whom He foreknew, He also predestined to be conformed to the image of His Son, that He might be the firstborn among many brethren" (Romans 8:28-29).

We do know that all things work together for good because we love God and we are called according to a purpose. We are not drifting through life without a compass. We have a compass: the Word of God. We understand that the wind that blows in our lives is not just the wind of adversity and the wind of chance, but also the wind of God. God is the one who takes my boat and by His breath, blows it in a certain direction. Yes, life *does* matter. Yes, life *does* work out according to God's will and plan.

Even when I believe and I do everything right, bad things still happen; I do not throw my hands up with a fatalistic, frustrated scowl and say, "What good is it anyway? There is no God in heaven and He does not know who I am!" This is what the devil would like this generation to do. We need to resist the fatalism mentality and attitude because it is a destructive force that the enemy is using in this generation.

The Fantasy Bondage

"Nothing is authentic; even Christian leaders are fake and churches are irrelevant. Therefore, I will live in my own make-believe world."

"Although they knew God, they did not glorify Him as God, nor were thankful, but became futile in their thoughts, and their foolish hearts were darkened" (Romans 1:21).

As Generation X-ers give in to the vain philosophies of man and the moral perversions of this culture, their thoughts will become more wicked and more futile, and their hearts will become darkened. This is the scheme of the wicked one to ruin this generation, to darken hearts and to close minds to the gospel by continually bombarding people with the thought that nothing is real or authentic; everything is synthetic, everything is relative and will pass away in time. There is nothing eternal about life or about man's soul. The Church cannot be trusted, leaders cannot be trusted, so we might as well live in any world we choose to make up for ourselves. The answer to life is to live as we please, getting any pleasures we want, without regard to any violations of our own morality or anyone else's. So, the enemy, by his spirit of darkness, is pushing this generation into a bondage of make-believe morality, of living in a fantasy world. These unreal fantasies offer no fulfillment, will never change lives, but only complicate and ruin them for the authentic reality of the gospel of Jesus Christ.

"For the weapons of our warfare are not carnal but mighty in God for pulling down strongholds, casting down arguments and any high thing that exalts itself against the knowledge of God, bringing every thought into captivity to the obedience of Christ, and being ready to punish all disobedience when your obedience is fulfilled" (II Corinthians 10:4-6).

We have a cure for this fantasy bondage, and that is to pull down every stronghold that the enemy has tried to establish in our minds. Believer or unbeliever, the enemy is after our minds. He seeks to distort our thoughts in such a way that we will not serve the living God nor acknowledge the truth that is taught in the Scriptures that Jesus Christ Himself has given us. The enemy seeks to confuse the minds of this generation that the unreal and the temporal will be trusted, not the authentic. Satan wants to make those things that are unreal, those things that have no life-giving power in them, the reality of people who do not trust the authentic. We cast down the bondage of addiction to fantasy in this generation, and we come against this with the truth of the Word of God. When everything else fails, the Word of God does not fail. The Word of God stands sure.

One is never bored who is serving the living God...

The Boredom Bondage

"Nothing excites me enough to be passionate; therefore I will do nothing."

Boredom is the brother of a slothful, lazy lifestyle. One is never bored who is serving the living God, serving His people and His purposes. As members of this generation sit amongst the rubble, fiddling with the remote control–the only way they know to effect change–boredom sets in, ruining the hearts of many. Boredom causes teenagers to begin to seek out fantasy because they are fed up with their own lives, fed up with the Church and fed up with God. Many people have put their lives on pause, some have put their lives on rewind and some have put their lives on fast-forward. The gospel of Jesus Christ puts lives on the right speed in the right direction.

We need to enjoy every day, and the way to enjoy life is not by serving self, but by serving and living for others. If we only serve and live for ourselves, we will die bored, senseless, selfish people. This is the strategy of the evil one to get people so wrapped up in their own problems and their own selves that they have no time to reach out and help someone else. The more we get wrapped up in ourselves and our own vain selfishness, the more we smother the emotions God has given us to be fulfilled through loving and serving others.

This generation has all the high-tech mobility and entertainment that any generation would ever want or ever need. Generation X-ers have everything at their fingertips to make them feel good, to entertain their minds and sensual appetites, and yet they are still bored. Why? Pleasures do not satisfy, speed of activity does not satisfy, possessions do not satisfy, career promotion and money do not satisfy. Even dissatisfaction causes boredom.

We can see an example of this with an athlete, one who may even be the best in the sports he participates in. Michael Jordan became bored with basketball, bored with being a superstar. He wanted to go out and conquer new mountains, different mountains. Even the Michael Jordans, or the best-paid actors, actresses, athletes or politicians in the world—if they do not serve others and live out the purposes of God, they will become bored with their lives. They might turn to drugs or alcohol or some other form of pleasure, or they may become workaholics, vainly trying to fulfill themselves because they are just bored with life.

The way to get un-bored is to establish new priorities, beginning with "Seek ye first the Kingdom of God and all these things will be added unto you." To seek first the Kingdom of God means to change your lifestyle and to adapt yourself to a Christ-like lifestyle. Christ said, "I came not to be served but to serve others. I came not to be ministered to, but to minister to others." Christ, the Son of God, showed us by example how to take a towel and basin to wash people's feet. Those who do not have the ability to wash feet have, also do not have the ability to enjoy life. If you want to rid yourself of boredom, clothe yourself with a servant's spirit. From that will come the excitement of Christian living and the excitement of life itself.

If you want to rid yourself of boredom, clothe yourself with a servant's spirit.

This generation is bored! What must we do? Give Generation X-ers more entertainment? Give them shorter church services? Give them shallower sermons? Give them no prayer life? Give them no worship? No power? No passion? When they darken the doors of the church, what will we give them?

We should give them power-packed preaching filled with the Word of God to challenge them to bear their crosses daily, give up their selfishness, repent of hedonistic lives that have no time for anyone else.

Why do so many men run off and leaving their families? Why do so many women want to fulfill their lives only in the career world? Because boredom has set into the life and heart of this culture. To turn this around, the true gospel of Jesus Christ must be preached, asking people for their lives, challenging them to give all to Christ and to begin to serve others in the humility of Christ. And people will respond, not because it makes sense to the human mind, but because it is the message of the gospel of Jesus Christ. It is the truth. If you will bear your cross daily, you will find your life. If you want to lose your life, serve yourself. If you want to find your life, serve the cross of Jesus Christ. The cross is what nails boredom.

The I-Am-Invisible Bondage

"Nothing I can do makes a difference now, and I doubt that I will ever make a difference."

This is an attitude that has set in and become deeply rooted in our society. People think that they are mistakes: "Why was I born anyway? I am so untalented. I am so un-everything. What life can I possibly have?" We have the answer for this generation. The best work that God has intended for this world has not even begun yet. Do not live in the shadow, but stretch forth into the light of God's Word. He who expects nothing shall never be disappointed.

The cure for this I-am-invisible bondage is to begin to preach the gospel of destiny and the gospel of the Kingdom, which says, "You have been chosen from the foundations of the world." You can make a difference. One praying person can make a difference. One true believing Christian can make a difference. One person with the power of the Holy Spirit living within him or her can change a generation, change the world.

From Generation X to Generation Destiny

As Gideon was turned around by the power of the Holy Spirit, so we can be turned around and turn our generation around. We do not have to let Generation X be named "Generation X." It has been called to be a generation of destiny, a generation that will be captured by the things of God, a generation that will make a difference in the world to come. This generation, I believe, will probably produce more leaders than my own generation of Baby Boomers. I believe this, despite the indications that so many minds in this younger generation have been captured by both the culture and Satanic strategy. But it is just in this kind of a situation that God arises and breaks the bonds off these young people, off these young leaders, and out of them will arise Gideons, Pauls and Davids who will turn the world upside down.

This generation is going to be reached by the gospel of Jesus Christ! Generation X is going to be transformed into "Generation Destiny." We will see Acts 13:36 come to reality with this generation:

...God is here to choose this generation!

"For David, after he had served his own generation by the will of God . . ." (Acts 13:36).

We have a vision for this generation, a vision that God wants to move in revival power upon the hearts and minds of young and old alike. I would pray that everyone who is reading these words right now would feel the urgency of the Holy Spirit in this day and age. I pray that right now in your own heart and mind you see yourself as a David, you see yourself as an Esther, you see yourself as one who is not disobedient to the heavenly vision, but obedient to the will of God for this generation.

"By faith Moses, when he became of age, refused to be called the son of Pharaoh's daughter" (Hebrews 11:24).

Refuse right now to be called the son or daughter of this world or this culture. Come of age. Be like Moses, and by faith accept the call of God for this day and for this generation.

Our call is clear. The time is now. We need to intercede and stand in the gap for this generation. 700 million are starving, 100 million live on the streets, millions are orphans and millions come from broken families. Our hearts must be moved with deep compassion, and intercession must be made continually. As we stand in the gap, let us intercede:

- That this generation will not be robbed of the spiritual revival God desires to send.
- That this generation will see the returning of godly values, godly convictions, and hunger for spiritual reality found only in Jesus.
- That this generation will experience a healing of mind, will and emotion, that trust would return, that faith would arise, that this generation would begin to put its hope in God, who cannot fail.
- That this generation would experience the godly ministry of spiritual mentors who will spiritually parent the young into maturity.
- That this generation would receive spiritual power to resist the deceiving works of the devil, resist occultism, New Age, drugs, alcohol, and pre-marital sex.

I have made such an effort to paint a graphic picture of the needs of this generation, the generation which is now becoming the future society of our nation and world, in order to stir hearts toward intercession with keen understanding. Now equipped with an understanding of the times, seasons, philosophy shifts and bondages of this generation, nation and world, let us proceed onward to our calling to become prayer-intercessors and stand in the gap!

Further Study

1. What are the bondage's gripping our nation today?

2. What is the Christian solution for cynicism? Fatalism? Boredom?

3. Does Generation X have a destiny? What should the Church's vision for Generation X be?

The Search
Enlisting Every Believer

Chapter Six:
Returning to Our First Call

As a young man walked along the beach every morning on his way to school, he would pass an old man standing on the beach, arms stretched out in prayer and intercession. Every afternoon as he headed home, the old man would still be standing there. Intrigued by this man's dedication and passion for prayer, he stopped one day and asked him, "Sir, will you teach me to pray like you?" The old man proceeded to grab the young man by his shirt, drag him into the ocean and push his head under water. He held the young man's head under the water and then pulled his head up. The boy gasped and filled his lungs with air just as the old man pushed his head back under the water for another minute. The old man pulled the boy's head back up again and allowed the boy to desperately grab a lung full of air.

Shocked, the young man asked him, "Why did you do that? All I did was ask you how to pray!" The old man looked at the boy and said, "Son, until you want God as badly as you just wanted air, I cannot teach you to pray."

Our first need is to desire God more than anything else in life. This desire motivates us to learn prayer, to deepen our spiritual roots.

Our First Call

Prayer-intercession is often lacking. It is the one thing that should come so naturally to Christians, yet it is neglected by many. When asked, almost every Christian will say he or she does not pray enough. Prayer can be the most powerful weapon in the Christian's arsenal, but often lies rusted and unused, last in his or her list of priorities. Most Christians in

America pray an average of seven minutes a day, while spending twenty-three hours a week in front of the television.

Prayer in the congregation is the root structure of the tree God wants to grow in His Church. Every upward growth must be balanced with an increased downward root system. This downward root increase is intensified prayer-intercession.

The words "pray," "prayer" or "praying" are used 530 times in the Bible. In the New Testament, one Scripture summarizes the four areas of prayer we need to look at:

"Therefore I exhort first of all that supplications, prayers, intercessions and giving of thanks be made for all men" (I Timothy 2:1).

There are seven Greek words for prayer in the New Testament, and four of them are used in this one verse. We shall examine the four. The Apostle Paul draws the attention of the Church to their primary purpose and focus. He simply states, "First of all," that this is a priority, the most essential part. When we give our energy to something, first of all, it should be to supplications, prayers, intercessions and giving of thanks.

If we are going to develop a program or strategy for reaching our communities, our cities or our nations, *first of all*, we need supplications, prayers, intercessions and giving of thanks. If we are having difficulty keeping our focus, if our passions are running low, our energies spent, *first of all*, we should give ourselves to supplications, prayers, intercessions and giving of thanks.

The first priority is prayer. Paul wrote this verse as a wake-up call for the body of Christ which Timothy, his son in the faith, was pastoring. He intended that their focus would remain on what is most powerful within the Kingdom of God, *first of all*, supplications, prayers, intercessions and giving of thanks. Acts 6:4 states our priority, "We will give ourselves continually to prayer and to the ministry of the word." The first priority is prayer. When this is adhered to, the book of Acts' results will be experienced.

For sake of continuity, I will cover the four words in this order: prayer, supplication, giving of thanks and, finally, intercession, which we will cover more comprehensively.

Prayer

The word "prayer" in the Greek is the word *proseuche*. This is the general word for prayer and worship unto God. This is a broad term, indicating a seeker of God in earnest devotion, and it is used thirty-seven times in the New Testament. A few verses in which this word is used are Matthew 21:13, 22; Mark 9:29; Luke 6:12, 22:45; Acts 1:14, 2:42, 3:1, 6:4, 10:4. When Paul exhorts this kind of praying, he is simply speaking about our communion with God. Prayer is the direct result of relationship with Christ and with the Holy Spirit. Without relationship, prayer becomes mere performance. There may be kneeling, standing, or bowing the head, yet there may not be any real praying.

When the heart is on fire with God Himself then prayer itself is on fire.

Prayer is from the heart. When the heart is on fire with God Himself, then prayer is on fire. Prayer must be filled with thoughts of God, words of God and passion for God. It is more feeling than words. Prayer is not a mere habit, recited by custom and memory. Prayer is not a duty. Prayer calls for heart. Here the apostle is calling the Church to a heart prayer, a seeking of God with passion.

Prayer is of the spirit, at times possesses the spirit and serves the spirit's high and holy purposes. Prayer is the channel through which all goodness flows from God to man and, eventually, all goodness from man to man. Prayer is a privilege, not a duty or an obligation. It is binding, and though it demands discipline and obedience, it is, first of all, a privilege that we can come before the throne of God and pray with heart. Prayer is a waiting upon God. Isaiah 40:31 says, "But those who wait on the Lord shall renew their strength; they shall mount up with wings like eagles, they shall run and not be weary, they shall walk and not faint."

When we pray with the spirit of prayer and with a passion of heart, prayer is the contact of a living soul with God. Prayer fills man's emptiness with God's fullness, man's poverty with God's riches, man's weakness with God's strength and man's smallness with God's greatness. Paul simply says that our first priority, our primary focus, is to give ourselves to be seekers of God. At the great events and crowning moments in the life of Jesus, we find Him in prayer. Jesus was a teacher of prayer by precept and example. His life was full of praying. Whole passages, parables and incidents were used by Christ to enforce the necessity and importance of prayer.

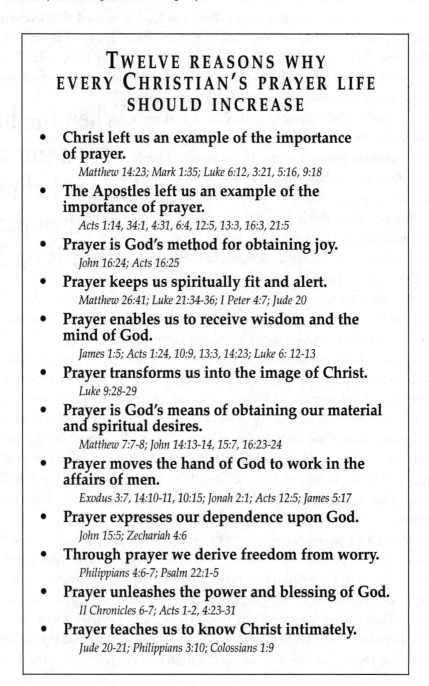

TWELVE REASONS WHY EVERY CHRISTIAN'S PRAYER LIFE SHOULD INCREASE

- **Christ left us an example of the importance of prayer.**
  Matthew 14:23; Mark 1:35; Luke 6:12, 3:21, 5:16, 9:18
- **The Apostles left us an example of the importance of prayer.**
  Acts 1:14, 34:1, 4:31, 6:4, 12:5, 13:3, 16:3, 21:5
- **Prayer is God's method for obtaining joy.**
  John 16:24; Acts 16:25
- **Prayer keeps us spiritually fit and alert.**
  Matthew 26:41; Luke 21:34-36; I Peter 4:7; Jude 20
- **Prayer enables us to receive wisdom and the mind of God.**
  James 1:5; Acts 1:24, 10:9, 13:3, 14:23; Luke 6: 12-13
- **Prayer transforms us into the image of Christ.**
  Luke 9:28-29
- **Prayer is God's means of obtaining our material and spiritual desires.**
  Matthew 7:7-8; John 14:13-14, 15:7, 16:23-24
- **Prayer moves the hand of God to work in the affairs of men.**
  Exodus 3:7, 14:10-11, 10:15; Jonah 2:1; Acts 12:5; James 5:17
- **Prayer expresses our dependence upon God.**
  John 15:5; Zechariah 4:6
- **Through prayer we derive freedom from worry.**
  Philippians 4:6-7; Psalm 22:1-5
- **Prayer unleashes the power and blessing of God.**
  II Chronicles 6-7; Acts 1-2, 4:23-31
- **Prayer teaches us to know Christ intimately.**
  Jude 20-21; Philippians 3:10; Colossians 1:9

The Prayer of Supplication

The second word Paul exhorts the believer to fulfill is the word "supplication." In the Greek, this is the word *deesis*, which means "a request, a petition which involves a begging, an intense seeking of God." This word describes the prayer of need and the prayer of request. It depicts the believer offering petitions to receive answers to needs. This is a prayer of greater earnestness and perseverance, a deeper petition than just the seeker-of-God prayers. Whether made to God or to man, it gives prominence to the expression of personal needs. In the Greek, the verb is *deomai*, wanting a need and asking to meet the need of a specific request. This Greek word is used nineteen times in the New Testament. It is translated "prayer" twelve times, "supplication" six times, and "request" one time. The word for supplications has within it at least three elements that are evident when this kind of praying takes place.

THREE ELEMENTS OF SUPPLICATION

- A plea for the return of the created order of life, which has apparently been hindered until now.

- A steadfast, continuous, and unceasing prayer indicating a tireless pursuit of a given goal.

- An intense, spiritual struggle, which will result in far-reaching ramifications for the whole work of the Kingdom of God.

Supplication is a strong, intense, spiritual kind of praying which brings specific results because of specific prayers. (See Luke 1:13, 2:37; II Corinthians 1:11, 9:14; Ephesians 6:18; Philippians 1:4,19, 4:6; II Timothy 1:3; Hebrews 5:7; James 5:16; I Peter 3:12.)

The son of a missionary to the Philippines tells of his introduction to true supplication:

Back of our home in the Philippines, during World War II, was the place where the Japanese tortured and killed their victims. We could hear the screams of the tortured day and night. Twice my father had been taken by enemy officers and returned to us as a result of my mother's supplications.

The third time the officer said, "He has been returned to you two times but don't you ever think he will be spared the third time. This time he dies." The officer left, taking my father with him. My mother put us children to bed on our grass mats and then began her prayer and supplication vigil for my father.

At 4:00 a.m. she awoke us, saying, "The burden has become so heavy I cannot bear it alone. Get up and help me pray for your father." We gathered in a circle around my mother with the two-month old baby on the floor in the center. While we were praying we heard footsteps. We were sure the officer was coming for us. Mother threw her arms around us as far as she could reach. Suddenly she said, "Those are your father's footsteps!"

We lit the lamp and saw his white shirt splattered with blood from those who stood near him. "I understand now why they let me go," he said soberly. "You were praying." He told us that he had been last in a row of ten men. A man had gone down the row with a sword, slashing off the head of each man. "He raised his sword as he came to me. Just as he was ready to bring it down, the officer in charge suddenly screamed, 'STOP!' Then the officer roared at me, 'Go home quick! Get out of here! Go home!' Then he dived at me, grabbed my arm and propelled me toward the gate and past the guard as fast as he could. And here I am."

That is what was happening at the time when mother was so burdened she got us up to pray. We don't know what the officer experienced to make him change the order, but we do know why. It was the prayers and supplications of our mother.[1]

The Prayer of Thanksgiving

The third kind of praying that the apostle exhorts the believer to is the giving of thanks. In the Greek this is the word *eucharistia*, that is, "a prayer with an attitude of thankfulness, praying with thanksgiving." It is the grateful acknowledgment of past mercies and is distinguished from the earnest seeking of future needs. It connotes returning thanks for blessings already received, which increases our faith and enables us to approach God with new boldness and new assurance. This is used often in the New Testament, fifteen times in total.

The following Scriptures contain this particular Greek word with the prayer of thanksgiving: Acts 24:3; I Corinthians 14:15-16, 9:11, 9:12; Ephesians 5:4; Colossians 2:7, 4:2; I Thessalonians 3:9; I Timothy 2:1, 4:3-4; Revelation 4:9, 7:12.

The Prayer of Intercession

The fourth word the Apostle exhorts us to practice is the word "intercession." The Greek word used in this particular text is the word *enteuxis*, which means "a prayer with a set meeting time, place and purpose." It means to mediate or to stand in for another. It is a free-flowing, bold prayer, prayed with child-like confidence.

Two other Greek words used for intercession in the New Testament are *entunchano*, which means "to fall in with, meet with in order to converse, to plead with a person with strong feelings." The other Greek word is *huperentenchano*, which means "to make a petition or intercede on behalf of another."

"Likewise the Spirit also helps in our weaknesses. For we do not know what we should pray for as we ought, but the Spirit Himself makes intercession for us with groanings which cannot be uttered. Now He who searches the hearts knows what the mind of the Spirit is, because He makes intercession for the saints according to the will of God" (Romans 8:26-27).

Ellicott, who was Bishop of Gloucester, England, in the nineteenth century and one of the great commentators, said intercession is "prayer in its most individual and urgent form, prayer in which God is, as it were, sought an audience and personally drawn nigh to."[2] The labor of prayer is to agree with God. This prayer begins in the heart of God. A.B. Simpson speaks of this word:

> This is more than seeking. It is not so much the prayer that knocks at the gates of heaven and extorts an answer from an unwilling God, as the prayer which, having received the answer of promise, carries it forth against the gates of the enemy and beats them down, as the walls of Jericho fell before the tramp and shout of Israel's believing hosts. It is faith putting its hand on the omnipotence of God and using it in fellowship with our own omnipotent Head until we see His name prevail against all that opposes His will, and the crooked things are made straight, the gates of brass are opened and the fetters of iron are broken asunder.[3]

Celia had ten children who were serving God, but the eleventh was running as fast as he could away from anything remotely connected with God. Day and night this prayer warrior poured out her heart in intercession for the life of her wayward son. Persistently, passionately, daily she cried out in prayer. Months passed and her son showed no sign of repentance until, one day, as he visited one of his brothers, her son began to pour out his frustrations and dissatisfactions with his life. He finally concluded, "My life is so miserable that I only have two choices. I either have to get right with God or get mother to stop praying. She'll never quit praying so I might as well get right with God."

Intensely, passionately and persistently knocking day and night at the gates of heaven, hammering away at the walls of Jericho, Celia prayed the prayer of supplication and intercession until the door opened, the walls fell, and her son was saved.

Hebrew words for Intercession

The first Hebrew word used for intercession is the word *palal* (used eighty-four times in the Old Testament), which means "to pray, to intervene, to mediate as a judge, to come between two parties." I Samuel 2:25 is a good example of this.

" 'If one man sins against another, God will judge him. But if a man sins against the Lord, who will intercede for him?' Nevertheless they did not heed the voice of their father, because the LORD desired to kill them" (1 Samuel 2:25).

The second Hebrew word is the word *paga*, which is used forty-four times in the Old Testament and means "to encounter, meet with, reach or stretch unto, to entreat, to strike, to touch, or to attack." In the Hebrew, it can be broken down into the *qal* or the *hiphil*. The *qal* of the Hebrew means "to meet, to light upon, to join, (used of kindness), to encounter, to fall upon (used of hostility), to encounter, to entreat (used of a request), or to strike, to touch (used of boundary)." Each one of these words will be broken down later in the book, and we will examine each meaning much more closely: "to fall upon," "to entreat" and also "to remove boundaries" or "to set boundaries." The *hiphil* usage in the Hebrew means "to cause to light upon, to cause to entreat, to make entreating, to interpose, to make attack, to reach the mark." The word *paga* is the broadest Hebrew word used for intercessory prayer.

Our First Call: Intercession

We, as the people of God, are being called to return to our first call, intercessory prayer.

One day a young man in Alexander the Great's army was caught running from the battle. As he was brought before Alexander, the lad responded with fear, "Sir, my name is Alexander." Filled with anger that this coward would share the same name as himself, Alexander demanded, "What did you say your name was?" Terrified, the lad answered, "My name is Alexander." Alexander the Great approached him and stared straight into his face. "Young man, either change your conduct or change your name."

...we, as Christians, are living in a season where we need to change our conduct or change our name.

Truly, we, as Christians, are living in a season in which we need to change our conduct or change our name. God has given us a priority call: a call to supplication, a call to prayer, a call to intercession, a call to giving of thanks. He exhorts us to fulfill this ministry, to take up this mighty weapon of prayer and intercession. We bear His name. Let us live in fulfillment of His call and bring honor to His name.

Further Study

1. Why is it important for every believer to be enlisted as an intercessor?

2. What are the different words for prayer mentioned in 1 Timothy 2:1? What do these words teach us about prayer?

3. What are the elements of supplication prayer?

4. What are the Hebrew words for intercession? What do these words teach us about prayer?

Notes

1.   <u>The Pentecostal Evangel</u>.

2.   Ellicott.

3.   A.B. Simpson.

Chapter Seven:
Marked for Intercession

A few years ago, there was a story in the newspaper of an experienced skydiving instructor who accompanied groups as they made their jumps, videotaping the jumps for them. One fateful day he bustled around the plane, assisting those who were jumping. As they approached the jump site, each person stepped out of the plane and began the free fall. The instructor followed them out the door and videotaped them as they rushed toward the ground. Then, one by one, they opened their parachutes. Video camera still running, the instructor reached for his cord only to discover that amidst the bustle of the pre-jump preparation, he had neglected to put on his parachute. All his years of experience and his expertise in skydiving were useless because of one moment of negligence.

Believers can busy themselves with the necessities of ministry, relying on their experience to enable them to minister effectively, only to discover that one area of negligence can destroy any effectiveness they may have. Intercession is easy to overlook in the busyness of ministry, but neglecting this area can be destructive.

Great Intercessors Define Intercession

The ministry of intercession can be defined not only through Greek and the Hebrew terms, but also conceptually by experience. Let us look at what other prayer warriors, authors and people involved in the ministry of intercession have said about it.

"Basically, intercession is prayer offered on behalf of another. When the prayer warrior intercedes, he forgets his personal needs and focuses all his faith and prayer attention on others. An intercessor is a man or woman or child who fights on behalf of others. As such, intercession is the activity that identifies us most with Christ. To be an intercessor is to be like Jesus because

History belongs to the intercessors.

that is what Jesus was like. He ever lives to intercede" (Dick Eastman).[1]

"Intercession can be a part of our lives now, the kind of prayer that works the impossible and sets new boundaries of possibility. The spirit of intercession is a bold understanding through prayer of whatever asserts itself against God's design for mankind. Holy Spirit begotten intercession forecasts new life, new hope and new possibilities for individuals in the impossible" (Jack Hayford).[2]

"Intercessory prayer is intensified praying which involves three special ingredients. Identification of the intercessor with the one whom is interceded for. Agony that feels the burden, the pain, the suffering, the need, and authority. This is the gained position of the intercessor to speak with authority that sees results" (Norman Grubb).[3]

"It is apparent that prayer lies close to the gift of the Holy Spirit. New Testament prayer was shown variously to be earnest, even opportunant, a matter of steadfastness and devotion. A day by day continuum of intercession. The church seen in the book of Acts was given over to the prayer of intercession with supernatural results" (*Renewal Theology*).[4]

"History belongs to the intercessors" (Walter Wink).[5]

"We are working with God to determine the future; certain things will happen in history if we pray right" (Richard Foster).[6]

"Intercessory prayer is an extension of the ministry of Jesus through His Body, the Church, whereby we mediate between God and humanity of the purpose of reconciling the world to Him, or between Satan and humanity for the purpose of enforcing the victory of Calvary" (Dutch Sheets).[7]

"Intercession is more than an occasional heartwarming, emotional love to God, more than expressions of goodwill on our knees. Prevailing prayer is holy work, fervent labor. You have no greater ministry or no leadership more influential than intercession. There is no higher role, honor, or authority than this" (Wesley Duevel).[8]

The Intercessory Ministry of the Church

The ministry of intercession is given to the Congregation, the Church as a whole, every person, every believer, the many-member Body of Christ. The gift of intercessory prayer is not a gift that can be found in just one or two people in the Church. It is a gift that has been imparted already to the entire Church. There will be those who have a burden and a ministry for more prayer and will develop the ministry of intercession to a fuller extent than others, but this does not mean that the gift of intercession actually resides in them, no more than the gift of prayer actually resides in some members of the Body of Christ, and not others. All members are called to pray. All members are called to intercede. All congregations are called to be interceding churches.

All members are called to intercede.

"I will build My church, and the gates of Hades shall not prevail against it" (Matthew 16:18). Other translations of this same portion of the verse state, "The power and forces of death shall never overpower the church and the locks of Sheol shall not shut on it and the power of the underworld shall never overthrow it and the gates of hell shall not hold out against it. The power and government of Hades will never be able to resist the church."

The church that moves in the authority delegated by Christ moves into the realm of intercessory prayer.

Opening the Gates Through Intercession

The function of gates is to keep things in, confine them, shut them up, control them. The gates of the council of darkness, the plots, ploys and plunderings of satanic origin are spawned in the spirit realm and erupt in the physical. These gates of hell will not be able to resist the moving of the Church in the spirit realm. The Church does not move against physical gates, because the Church is not physical. It does not fight against physical beings, because the Church itself is a spiritual entity. Our battle rests not in flesh and blood, but against wickedness in high places, against principalities and powers, against demonic forces, against the power and forces of death and hell. As we come against the gates of hell, we come against the authority of hell–the gates speak of authority. Our job as the Church is to open the gates. (See Isaiah 26:2, 60:11.)

"And I will give you the keys of the kingdom of heaven, and whatever you bind on earth will be bound in heaven, and whatever you loose on earth will be loosed in heaven" (Matthew 16:19).

Using the Keys of Spiritual Authority

The keys are given to the Church to stop hell's worst, to unlock prison doors and to shatter Satan's chains. Keys represent the authority one has to enter certain domains. God has given the Church the right to function in the domain of the Almighty.

To bind is to move into a realm of intercessory prayer, or to intercede. "Bind" is the Greek word *deses*. "Supplication" is the Greek word *deesis*. As you can see, these two words are from the same Greek family. To supplicate or to bind is the same work in the realm of the Holy Spirit. In Matthew 12, Jesus says that we cannot enter into a strongman's house and plunder his goods unless we first bind the strongman. Binding is contracting with God through intercessory prayer, saying, "Father, what You have willed, I call forth on earth." Binding is a steadfast continuity of regular and unceasing prayers, indicating a timeless pursuit of a given goal. Binding is an intense spiritual struggle, the issue of which will determine with far-reaching effect the whole work of the Kingdom of God.

> **It is absolutely necessary that the entire congregation be motivated toward intercessory prayer.**

"Whatever you bind [*deesis*], whatever you may at any time encounter of hell's councils, which I am declaring my church shall prevail against, you will then face a decision as to whether you will or won't bind it. What transpires will be conditional upon your response. If you do personally and consciously involve yourself in the act of binding the issue on earth, you will discover at that future moment when you do that it has already been bound in heaven" (Jack Hayford).[9]

The Church has been given the keys of heaven, and whatever is bound on earth shall be bound. As we see, the binding ministry is one aspect of the intercessory prayer ministry. It is absolutely necessary that the entire congregation be motivated toward the ministry of intercessory prayer. This Greek word *deesis*, that is, supplication, is translated in the

New Testament as "prayer" in Luke 1:13, 2:37, 5:33 and several other places where prayer and fasting are linked together, as supplication and binding are linked together.

Again, intercession is not the responsibility for a few designated or called-to-be intercessors, but it is the overall job description of the entire Church of the Lord Jesus.

Intercession can mean making a difference, even in the worst of cases. Even death and life can be affected. Drs. Will and Charles Mayo from the world-famous May Clinic said, "I have seen patients that were dead by all standards. We knew that they could not live, but I have seen a minister come in to the bedside and do something that I could not do although I had done everything in my professional power. But something touched some immortal spark in him and, in defiance of medical knowledge and materialistic common sense, that patient lived."

As intercessors prayed with authority, calling for God's will in heaven to bear upon the situation on earth, life triumphed over death.

Every Believer is Responsible for Prayer-Intercession

For the Church to move forward into the ministry of intercessory prayer, the entire congregation must take this as a responsibility. Every believer must say these words: "I am responsible. This is my ministry. I have been called to intercession." (See Isaiah 56:7.)

"And the Lord said to him, 'Go through the midst of the city, through the midst of Jerusalem, and put a mark on the foreheads of the men who sigh and cry over all the abominations that are done within it' " (Ezekiel 9:4).

The word "mark" in the Hebrew is the word *tau*, which when written in the Hebrew appears like a cross. The mark put on the forehead of each person was the sign of the cross; and the sign of the cross was put upon those who had the ability to sigh and cry over the sin of abomination going on in the city. This, again, is another form of intercession: those who have the burden and the ability to stand in the gap for the city, who realize that degenerate sin will cause the city to be destroyed.

Intercession is the responsibility of every believer in every city for every nation.

Today, the Holy Spirit desires to put the mark of the cross upon all believers. The mark of the cross is the mark of intercession because the Lord Jesus lives to make intercession for us. He is the Chief Intercessor, so His Congregation is a Congregation of intercessors with a mark on their foreheads. Their passions, their energies, their mindsets are toward the ministry of intercession. Intercession is not a spiritual gift, but it can be a calling, and all who are in the Congregation of the righteous are called to this Christian discipline. Intercession is the responsibility of every believer of every church in every city for every nation.

"He saw that there was no man, and wondered that there was no intercessor; therefore His own arm brought salvation for Him; and His own righteousness, it sustained Him" (Isaiah 59:16).

Further Study

1. Who in the church is gifted with intercessory prayer? Is this a gift given only to the few?

2. Is it the task of the church to open gates (Matthew 16:19)? Specifically, what does this mean in terms of binding and loosing?

3. What can we learn about the responsibility for intercession from Isaiah 56:7, Ezekiel 9:4, and Isaiah 59:16?

Notes

1.   Dick Eastman, The Hour that Changes the World (Grand Rapids, MI: Baker Book House, 1978), 76-77

2.   Jack Hayford, Invading the Impossible (Logos International, 1977), 125.

3.   Norman Grubb, Rees Howells Intercessors (Christian Literature, 1973).

4.   Renewal Theology.

5.   Walter Wink.

6.   Richard Foster, Celebration of Discipline.

7.   Dutch Sheets, Intercessory Prayer (Ventura, CA: Regal Books, 1996).

8.   Wesley Duevel, Mighty Prevailing Prayer (Grand Rapids: Zondervan, 1990), 20-22.

9.   Jack Hayford, Invading the Impossible.

Chapter Eight:
Exposing the Myths of Intercession

The word "myth" speaks of a legend, traditional story or fiction. It is a product of imagination only. It is not real or true, but fictitious. Just as their are cultural and historical myths, so also there are myths about intercessory prayer.

Today, the Holy Spirit is moving congregations into the ministry of intercession and is taking it out of the hands of the specialists, or those who have actually given themselves to only this ministry in times past. Intercession is not meant to be just for the retired missionary, some fanatical saints, or certain women who perhaps have the time for a morning prayer meeting during the week. Thank God for the retired missionaries and the women who, in times past, have given themselves to more prayer. But this ministry must be elevated to the place where it is for the entire congregation, not just for a few people on a part-time basis. It must not be shoved off into a corner or a closet or a spare room somewhere. Intercession must be brought front and center into the

I am responsible. This is my ministry. I am called to be an intercessor.

congregational public meetings, in the Sunday morning meetings, the Sunday night meetings and special nights when the church is called to intercede. Intercession is something the children, the young people, the young adults, the young marrieds, the middle-aged, the old and the retired must all experience. Every believer's spirit must say, "I am responsible. This is my ministry. I am called to be an intercessor."

"You have not gone up into the gaps to build a wall for the house of Israel to stand in battle on the day of the Lord" (Ezekiel 13:5).

This indictment could apply to many believers who fail to intercede out of ignorance, complacency, apathy or lack of spiritual motivation. Many believers and churches have not gone into the gaps, built walls or stood in battle on the day of the Lord because they have handed this ministry over only to those who have that "gifting" and actually give themselves to it. This is a spiritual cop-out.

We are all called to the ministry of standing in the gap, building the hedge and standing in the battle for the world to be saved, for the enemy to be defeated, for nations to have open heavens so that the Holy Spirit may move. When the Lord looks down upon my home, He will not say, let Him not say, "I wonder that there was no intercessor," or "Why have you not gone to stand in the gap or to build a hedge? Why were you not involved with the battle?" But let Him look down upon every family in the congregation and say, "There are intercessors in that home, people who understand their spiritual responsibility, and they have a mark on their foreheads, the mark of the cross, the mark of true discipleship."

Myth 1: "It is a spiritual gift for a selected few."

We must, first of all, biblically disprove this. We must seek spiritual understanding, for this has become a common misconception. Is there a pattern in the book of Acts or in the Epistles or in the Gospels, indicating that this is only for a selected few? In my research I have found that there is no spiritual gift entitled "Intercessory Prayer." It can be a calling and a ministry, but that calling and ministry is not singled out for a few. Rather, it has been given to the entire congregation.

Myth 2: "It is a level of prayer that I can never reach."

Many people are discouraged when they hear teaching on interces-sion, and they immediately excuse themselves based on their present devotional prayer life. They hear stories about intercessors who spend one, two, three or four hours a day interceding, or about the intensity or the volume of the prayer, and they immediately dismiss it, saying, "I can never give that much time or that much intensity to this level of prayer called intercession." And so they excuse themselves based on stories and testimonies. Now, there are people who spend hours and there are people who have levels of intensity far beyond others, but that should not cause us to excuse ourselves and elevate others. We are all called to a certain level of intercession.

Myth 3: "I would never have the time."

Again, the stories that come before the congregation, the articles that are handed out, the different testimonies that are given about the amount of time that must be spent in order to have impact in the Kingdom of God through intercession will cause those who pray only by the minute to dismiss the hourly praying as that rigorous kind of prayer allotted only for the select intercessor. All of us have time. We need to make time and take responsibility for intercessory prayer.

Myth 4: "I do not have the personality for that kind of praying."

The assumed personality for a prayer warrior or an intercessor seems to be an intense individual who is monastic, isolated, non-sociable, interested only in the prayer room. But again, this is not the true nature of the intercessor as seen in Scripture. We must not look at the personalities of people we have elevated as intercessors and derive our definition and job description for intercessors based on those people. We must look to the Scripture. All personalities must submit to the working of the Holy Spirit. All personalities must submit to the Word of God.

Our personalities do not have dominion over our ministries or our function in the Body of Christ. Our personalities must be purged from carnality and selfishness in being timid and intimidated. These things must be purged out of our old selves so that we can function as prayer warriors in the House of God.

Myth 5: "Isn't this for retired missionaries, elderly women and fanatic saints?"

Just because many retired missionaries and elderly women have been intercessors in the past does not mean that those are the only people God has called and wants to work with. Yes, there are people who have more time or maybe have a greater burden because of their past history of ministry and experience. They know the power of prayer, so they have given themselves to prayer.

If you give yourself to prayer, you will become a prayer warrior. If you give yourself to witnessing, you will become a person who wins souls. If you give yourself to study, you will become more knowledgeable. One must give himself to something in order for that thing to be developed in his or her life. We will never give ourselves to intercessory prayer if we believe that it is a spiritual gift we do not possess and if we are waiting for some kind of a "magic wand" to make us feel divine motivation toward the intercessory prayer ministry. Again, I am not minimizing those people who develop maturity in this area of ministry. I am simply stating that I do not see a New Testament principle asserting that intercession is given to only a few people.

Dr. C. Peter Wagner, in his book, *Your Spiritual Gifts Can Help Your Church Grow*, deals with the gift of intercession. He states, "Certain Christians, it seems to me, have a special ability to pray for extended periods of time on a regular basis and see frequent and specific answers to their prayers to a degree much greater than that which is expected of the average Christian. This is the gift of intercession."[1]

He deals with the gift of intercession from the standpoint of his experience with people around him or people he has read about who have the ability to spend a lot of time in intercession. I am not at all negating my good friend's work on spiritual gifts or his books on prayer. I am simply stating that the gift of intercession is a gift given to the entire Church. Every believer has within himself the holy spirit of intercession because Christ dwells within us all and He is the Chief Intercessor.

There are those who will develop this God-given ability more than others and who will eagerly embrace it, but this does not excuse other people from actually developing the ministry of intercession to the level that the Church must have in order to bind, loose and resist darkness in every region of the world.

Myth 6: "What difference can one prayer make?"

As we succumb to cynicism or fatalism, of course, the devil will manipulate and magnify it until we become discouraged with our praying. We actually feel that one person cannot make a difference and, therefore, if we do not pray, even though we could pray about certain things, it really will not change anything in the Kingdom of God or the kingdom of darkness.

Of course, this is a lie, and the enemy enlarges and magnifies this lie continually until it becomes a stronghold in the mind of every praying person. Throughout Scripture we see, time after time, that one person has made a difference, from Abraham right on down to the Apostle Paul.

Each time one person has stood in the gap, has built a hedge or stood on the day of battle, God has moved in miraculous ways. God only needs someone to harness with Him, partner with Him concerning anything he or she wishes to touch in prayer; and the mighty hand of God can move in ways that are far beyond human reasoning or human imagination.

We must rid ourselves of all man-made myths and Satanic plots to destroy the ministry of intercession in the Congregation of the Lord Jesus Christ.

"I will build My church, and the gates of Hades shall not prevail against it" (Matthew 16:18).

Standing Firm in the Truth

We are the Church; we are the *ekklesia*. This Greek word *ekklesia* was also used in New Testament times to refer to political assembly. The assembly consisted of the citizens of a Greek city. In this connection, *ekklesia*, translated as "assembly," occurs many times in the New Testament. The assembly, or the *ekklesia*, in this incident in the New Testament, obviously conveys the concept of coming together. The regular assembly refers more to official occasions than unofficial. The word *ekklesia* connotes being called from our regular activities and ordinary responsibilities into the *ekklesia*. This carries with it the dynamic and active sense of a people called for a particular purpose and activity.

The Church is the assembly of the called and consists of those who have been called out. The word *ek* in the Greek means 'out' and the word *kaleo* is the word 'called.' Hence, the Church is composed of called-out people. The Church has been called out, not only from ordinary responsibilities, but also from the darkness of our past sin and evil. Thus, God has called the Church out of darkness into His marvelous light. This calling, among other things, is for us to be a people of intercession. Every believer is a New Testament priest who willingly and consistently offers up prayer incense. (See Exodus 19:5-6; Matthew 21:43; II Timothy 1:9.)

"But you are a chosen generation, a royal priesthood, a holy nation, His own special people, that you may proclaim the praises of Him who called you out of darkness into His marvelous light" (I Peter 2:9).

The Church by definition consists of those called out of the world, delivered, saved, sanctified–whatever terminology is needed to describe that transition from darkness to light–and into a place of decision-making and extending the Kingdom of God. In Matthew 16:18 when Jesus says, "I will build My church," He refers to it as His own possession. Thus, the Church belongs to Him. He is the builder, and to Him total obedience is due.

So when the Lord Jesus states that the job description of the Church is to bind (and we have already discovered that the word *bind* and the word *intercession* belong together), this carries a high calling for the *ekklesia*. Intercessory prayer is one of the main purposes of the Church. The church is called to various functions, many of which are very familiar to many congregations in the world today. Other functions are much less familiar.

The Church's first responsibility is to the ministry of supplication and intercession.

The Church is called to worship with praise and adoration, uplifting the name of the Lord in each congregation. The style may be different, but the spirit of worship is necessary for Christ to dwell in our midst. We understand that the Church is called to function in the realm of worship, evangelism, teaching, equipping, church planting, missions endeavors. But its first responsibility is to the ministry of supplication and intercession.

"Therefore I exhort first of all that supplications, prayers, intercessions, and giving of thanks be made for all men, for kings and all who are in authority, that we may lead a quiet and peaceable life in all godliness and reverence" (I Timothy 2:1).

We are God's chosen priests, chosen to specifically fulfill the ministry of prayer-intercession. Professionally, we may be schoolteachers, carpenters, engineers, secretaries, businessmen or businesswomen. This is how we support our calling as priests. Our real purpose in life is to fulfill this high calling of prayer. Christianity is not a spectator sport played by the professionals. The clergy are not the only players; they are not the only pray-ers. All of us have the responsibility and privilege to storm the gates of hell, bring down spiritual powers in high places, and set the captives free. We are God's hands, feet and mouth. Let us not accept myths as an excuse. We are called to powerful intercession!

PRAYER

Oh God, let us, Your people, reject these myths about intercession and instead return to our first call, our first priority, our first love–prayer-intercession made continually by all believers. We bend our knees with a humble heart and cry aloud with one heart and one voice, for we are Your Church. We recognize our authority to destroy the gates and powers of hell and use this authority now, in our day, for our generation.

Further Study

1. Why do many believers fail to intercede? What are the myths concerning intercession?

2. Do any of the myths of intercession apply to your own life? How should you respond to these myths?

3. What does it mean to be the ekklesia? What does being part of the church have to do with intercession?

Note

1. Dr. C. Peter Wagner, <u>Your Spiritual Gifts Can Help Your Church Grow</u>.

Chapter Nine:
Searching for Willing Intercessors

John Hyde, a missionary to India, made prayer his first priority. The evidence was seen in his life to such an extent that he became known as "Praying Hyde." Dr. Wilbur Chapman wrote to a friend about his encounter with this man of prayer:

> I have learned some great lessons concerning prayer. In one of our missions in England the audience was exceedingly small, but I received a note saying that an American missionary was going to pray for God's blessing down on our work. He was known as Praying Hyde. Almost instantly the tide turned. The hall became packed and at my first invitation fifty men accepted Christ as their Savior. As we were leaving I said, "Mr. Hyde, I want you to pray for me." He came to my room, turned the key in the door and dropped on his knees and waited five minutes without a single syllable coming from his lips. I could hear my own heart thumping and his beating. I felt hot tears running down my face. I knew I was with God. Then, with an upturned face, while the tears were streaming, he said, "Oh God!" Then for five minutes, at least, he was still again. Then when he knew that he was talking with God, there came from the depths of his heart such petitions for me as I had never heard before. I rose from my knees to know what real prayer was. We believe that prayer is mighty and we believe it as we never did before.[1]

I have endeavored to establish a biblical mindset toward the ministry of intercession. I have established that the priority and the most essential element in Christ's Church is intercessory prayer. This foundational stone is absolutely necessary if the entire Congregation, all of God's people, in any given locality, are to become an interceding community with an interceding conviction. This is a selah, a check point, a pivotal point in our journey.

Each believer is a member of an occupational force which has one principal purpose: to enforce the victory won at Calvary through all methods available, especially using intercessory prayer. More than a simple, single-dimensional asking, intercession becomes a multi-faceted weapon through supplication, intercessory prayer, warfare, praise and worship.

"Therefore I exhort first of all that supplications, prayers, intercessions, and giving of thanks be made for all men" (I Timothy 2:1).

Restoring Our First Love and Our First Call

The first call develops along with our initial love relationship to Christ through the Holy Spirit. When our first love waivers, our first call will falter. We are exhorted as people of God to maintain a hot heart, full of passion for God. Out of this love and passion the prayer of intercession flows. Then we shall be like Elizabeth as stated in Luke 2:37, "And this woman was a widow of about eighty-four years, who did not depart from the temple, but served God with fastings and prayers night and day."

This is a picture of a love relationship in intercessory prayer. Prayer is to fill our lives, saturate us, as the altar of incense was saturated with the sweet aroma of burning incense. Christ's life was a constant stream of incense, sweet and perfumed by passionate prayer. So also, the Church of the twenty-first century is being saturated with this prayer aroma.

Let us now venture into a section of Scripture that is quoted quite often when discussing intercessory prayer. The key Scripture is Ezekiel 22:30, but we will study the context of Ezekiel 22:13-30.

" 'So I sought for a man among them who would make a wall, and stand in the gap before Me on behalf of the land, that I should not destroy it; but I found no one. Therefore I have poured out My indignation on them; I have consumed them with the fire of My wrath; and I have recompensed their deeds on their own heads,' says the Lord God" (Ezekiel 22:30-31).

This portion of Scripture establishes a powerful biblical principle: the awesome power of intercessory prayer to **hold back destruction**

upon the land and, instead, **bring healing, revival and restoration.**
The force of one person, group or groups of people willing to pay the
price to stand in the gap is staggering. We need intercessory leaders
who will nurture interceding prayer teams, who will build interceding
churches that will intercede for cities,
nations and the whole world, thus shaping history for global revival.

Pursuit of God

Ezekiel 22:30 begins with the pursuit of
God, "So I sought." The word "sought" in
the Hebrew connotes a person earnestly
seeking something which, or someone who,
exists or is thought to exist. Its intention is
that its object be found or acquired.

God is determined to discover intercessors. He is pursuing, with His divine power

> The awesome power of intercessory prayer holds back destruction upon the land and instead brings healing, revival and restoration.

and might, seeking to find intercessory prayer functioning powerfully and
regularly amongst His called-out people, His Church. (See Jeremiah 27:18.)

"He saw that there was no man, and wondered that there was no
intercessor; therefore His own arm brought salvation for Him; and His
own righteousness, it sustained Him" (Isaiah 59:16).

God's Search for Willing Vessels

Ezekiel 22:30 also states that God's pursuit is "for a man." "God plus
one equals a majority" is a biblical truth. God is seeking one person, one
Church, one city-church to turn the tide and reshape history. One pastor,
one evangelist, one teacher, one housewife, one businessperson, one
teenager standing in his or her generation, one policeman or woman. Just
one. One in every sphere of life, one in every office building, school
facility or neighborhood. Just one!

One such as Ryan, a senior in high school, who, frustrated with the drugs
and violence in his high school, decided to pray. Every morning he stood at
the flagpole and prayed for the school. In five months he saw over fifty-five
people saved, the beginning of a significant revival in his high school. It was
all due to one young man being a willing vessel to stand in the gap.

One such as Esther, one faithful Jew alone among the Gentiles, who
had no army to call upon to save her people. All the Jews across the

nation were waiting in terror for the day when their enemies would attack. They even knew the exact day it would come, since King Ahasureus had issued a decree "to destroy, to kill and to annihilate all the Jews, both young and old, little children and women, in one day, on the thirteenth day of the twelfth month" (Esther 3:13). It was law, a law that could not be changed. There was no hope.

Yet God had placed this young girl in a position of readiness to stand in the gap. She had been "drafted" by the king to be his queen. It was a position without power. Yet, she could not even approach him without a special invitation and he had not bothered to give her a call for a month. What could she do, one young girl alone against the inflexible laws of Persia and the wrath of a king?

With fasting and prayer Esther stood in the gap.

She took to heart the words of Mordecai, her uncle, "Who knows but that you have come to the kingdom for such a time as this." (See Esther 4:14.) With fasting and prayer Esther stood in the gap. She stood alone between a king and her people and pleaded their cause. She stood alone and changed the course of history for her people.

"God shapes the world by prayer; the prayers of God's saints are the capitol stock of heaven by which God carries on His great work upon earth" (E.M. Bounds).[2]

"Oh, that one might plead for a man with God, as a man pleads for his neighbor!" (Job 16:21).

"God does nothing but in answer to prayer" (John Wesley).[3]

In every generation, in every nation, in every city, God has a person, a man or woman, who is responding to the call of the Spirit to stand in the gap, turn the tide and shape history. Intercessory prayer is striking the winning blow at the precise moment in time when the battle is the hottest. God is seeking intercessors. He will not relent, He will not draw back and He will not be disappointed. God is visiting His people with His awesome holy presence. God is filling His house with His glory. Isaiah 6:1-8 states that God is visiting His man, His intercessor, His hope for the nation. Isaiah's response is much like our response to God's visitation.

"So I said: 'Woe is me, for I am undone! Because I am a man of unclean lips, and I dwell in the midst of a people of unclean lips; for my eyes have seen the King, the Lord of hosts' " (Isaiah 6:5).

Even though we are overwhelmed with our sinfulness and our unclean lips, God, by His grace, visits our mouth with a live coal from the altar. Could this be the altar of incense in heaven? Could these live coals be the passion and fire we need to pray with the fire of God as intercessors? The coal touches the mouth, the lips, the prayer vehicle. Isaiah hears the cry of the heart of God, "Whom shall I send, and who will go for us?" He responds, "Here am I, send me!"

God seeks for intercessors. Here I am, send me! God is in desperate need for a man or a woman to stand in the gap, build the hedge. Here am I, use me!

God's Search for Intercessors

Ezekiel 22:30 goes on to say, "I sought for a man among them."

GOD SEARCHED AMONG THE...

Priests

Ezekiel 22:26: "Her priests have violated My law and profaned My holy things . . ."

The priests were trained to stand between God and man, to make atonement for sins, to offer sacrifices on behalf of each person, each family and ultimately the nation.

Princes

Ezekiel 22:27: "Her princes in her midst are like wolves tearing the prey, to shed blood, to destroy people, and to get dishonest gain."

The princes were those who had the position and responsibility to lead the people of God in all aspects of life.

People

Ezekiel 22:29: "The people of the land have used oppressions, committed robbery, and mistreated the poor and needy; and they wrongfully oppress the stranger."

He sought among them, city by city, town by town, village by village, house by house, slowly, carefully, thoroughly. Where are they? But He found none!

Prophets

Ezekiel 22:28: "Her prophets plastered them with untempered mortar, . . . Thus says the Lord God,' when the Lord had not spoken."

When God sought for intercessors, of course He would seek them among the prophets, but the search was in vain.

Who are the "them" referred to in this verse? Whoever they were, they had the potential of turning the wrath of God away from destroying the land and, instead, ushering in healing and revival. They failed. The "them" were totally given over to everything but intercessory prayer.

The context reveals those who made up this group that God had diligently searched, seeking to find His intercessors. His search was in vain. This verse ends by stating, "but I found no one." Astounding to believe or to imagine that God, with all His power and ability to search for someone or something, would come up with nothing, no one–zip, zero, a blank, not one soul. What people could have failed God and their nation so pathetically, so completely?

Ezekiel 22:26-29 reveals the four groups of people that make up the "them" of Ezekiel 22:30: the priests, the princes, the prophets and, finally, the people.

Priests

"Her priests have violated My law and profaned My holy things; they have not distinguished between the holy and unholy, nor have they made known the difference between the unclean and the clean; and they have hidden their eyes from My Sabbaths, so that I am profaned among them" (Ezekiel 22:26).

The priests were the most obvious group in which to search. They were employed by God through the people's tithes and offerings to do the work of intercession, prayer, worship and teaching. They were obviously trained to be ready at all times to do the work of intercession. The priests were trained to stand between God and man, to make atonement for sins, to offer sacrifices on behalf of each person, each family and ultimately the nation. (See Leviticus 4:3-7, 10-17, 20-35, 14:1-48, 15:14-15, 16:30-32, 17:5-6; Deuteronomy 20:2; Ezra 2:63; Nehemiah 8:2, 9.)

Princes

"Her princes in her midst are like wolves tearing the prey, to shed blood, to destroy people, and to get dishonest gain" (Ezekiel 22:27).

The princes were those who had the position and responsibility to lead the people of God in all aspects of life. A prince had power with God and with man. (See Genesis 32:28.) Each tribe of Israel had its own princes, each holding different levels of rank within his tribe. (See Numbers 7:18-24, 30, 36, 42, 48, 54, 60, 66, 72, 78.) In Numbers 16:1-2, we see 250 princes of Israel, called "representatives of the congregation," men of respect and renown. These princes had influence, power and authority, with God and the congregation. (See Numbers 34:18; Joshua 22:14; II Samuel 3:38.) This group could easily have called the nation to repentance by being a model of repentance through intercessory prayer, standing in the gap for the sins of the people and building spiritual hedges to protect the people of God.

Prophets

"Her prophets plastered them with untempered mortar, seeing false visions, and divining lies for them, saying, 'Thus says the Lord God,' when the Lord had not spoken" (Ezekiel 22:28).

The prophets were those who had the privilege and responsibility of hearing from God and speaking for God to the people. Prophets were called to be men of prayer. Genesis 20:7 states that Abraham was a prophet and He would pray the prayer of restoration and God would hear Him. Aaron was a prophet for Moses to stand between God and man and between Moses and the congregation. (See Exodus 7:1.)

The prophets were used by God to turn the hearts of the people, to rebuke sin, to keep the nation from idolatry, immorality and backsliding. (See Numbers 12:6; Deuteronomy 13:1-5, 18:15-22; Isaiah 3:20, 2, 9:9, 28:7; Jeremiah 1:5; Hosea 12:13-14.) The prophets were to be intercessors. They were anointed for their office; they had divine gifts to see into the spirit realm. God Himself guided their words and gave them dreams and visions.

The prophets failed. They were prophesying for money, prestige and material gain. They were giving false visions, telling lies, speaking what the people wanted to hear. But God had not spoken. When God sought for intercessors, of course He would seek them among the prophets, but the search was in vain.

People

"The people of the land have used oppressions, committed robbery, and mistreated the poor and needy; and they wrongfully oppress the stranger" (Ezekiel 22:29).

God had gone to the obvious groups, searching for intercessors. He had visited the priests, the princes and the prophets. Finally He turned to the largest group to seek an intercessor. There were thousands of priests, hundreds of princes, tens of prophets. This time He went to the millions, the entire nation, the people.

The people had become like their leadership, sinful and enjoying their sin. (See Hosea 4:9.) There was no repentance in the top leadership, so there could be no repentance in the people. They were engrossed in their selfish, sinful, small lifestyles. God sought among them, city by city, town by town, village by village, house by house, slowly, carefully, thoroughly. Seeking for intercessors, men, women, children. Who are they? Where are they? But He found none! The whole nation had become spiritually bankrupt, hardened, with no one to hear God seeking for gap standers.

"So I sought for a man among them who would make a wall, and stand in the gap before Me on behalf of the land, that I should not destroy it; but I found no one" (Ezekiel 22:30).

God Is Still Seeking

Dr. Alexander Duff was a great, longtime missionary to India. When he was an old man, he returned to his homeland of Scotland to die. There, during the general assembly of the Church of Scotland, Dr. Duff addressed the meeting and then made a strong appeal for young people to volunteer their lives for India, but no one responded. Under the strain of the appeal, the aged missionary fainted and fell to the floor and was carried off the platform. The doctor bent over the old veteran and was examining his heart, when he suddenly opened his eyes and asked, "Where am I now? Where am I?" "Lie still," urged the physician, "your heart is very weak." The old warrior interrupted, "But I must finish my appeal! Take me back! Take me back! I have not finished my appeal yet!" Again the doctor cautioned, "Lie still. You are too weak to go back." But the missionary would not be stopped. Gathering his strength he got back on his feet and, with the doctor on one side and the assembly chairman on the other, the great white-haired warrior was led back to the pulpit. While the whole congregation rose in honor of his courage, he then resumed his appeal.

"When Queen Victoria calls for volunteers for India, hundreds of young men respond. But when King Jesus calls, no one goes." Then he paused. Once more he continued, "Is it true that Scotland has no more sons to give for India?" Then he waited. Still no one responded. There was silence. The old man then made a major decision. Under the heavy burden of India's un-reached millions, he concluded his call, "Very well. If Scotland has no more young men to send to India, then old and decrepit though I am, I will go back. Even though I cannot preach, I can lie down on the shores of the Ganges River and die in order to let the people of India know that there is at least one man in Scotland who cares enough for their souls to give his life for them." As the old veteran turned to leave the pulpit, finally the silence was broken. All over the congregation young men got to their feet and cried, "I'll go! I'll go!" After old Dr. Duff passed on, many of those young men did go to India, investing their lives as a result of an old gospel warrior's burden, love and vision for the lost people of India.

Much like Dr. Duff, God is crying out, "Is there anyone who will intercede? Is there anyone who will give his or her life for My people? Is there anyone who will join My army of prayer warriors?"

Today, God is still seeking among "them" for His army of prayer warriors and Holy Spirit-propelled intercessors. Priests may fail, princes may fail, prophets may fail, but God will raise up a remnant of His people. We are the people of God.

> **Is there anyone who will join My army of prayer warriors?**

(See II Corinthians 6:16.) As the interceding Church, we are called to stand in the gap. As we respond to the Spirit's call to become a people of intercessory prayer, we will seek to fulfill the prayer responsibility stated in Ezekiel 22:30-31.

Gap Standing Intercessors

Esther

"Then Esther told them to reply to Mordecai: 'Go, gather all the Jews who are present in Shushan, and fast for me; neither eat nor drink for three days, night or day. My maids and I will fast likewise. And so I will go to the king, which is against the law; and if I perish, I perish!' " (Esther 4:15-16). (See Esther 5:1-3.)

Elijah

"Then Elijah said to Ahab, 'Go up, eat and drink; for there is the sound of abundance of rain.' So Ahab went up to eat and drink. And Elijah went up to the top of Carmel; then he bowed down on the ground, and put his face between his knees, and said to his servant, 'Go up now, look toward the sea.' So he went up and looked and said, 'There is nothing.'

And seven times he said, 'Go again.' Then it came to pass the seventh time that he said, 'There is a cloud, as small as a man's hand, rising out of the sea!' So he said, 'Go up, say to Ahab, "Prepare your chariot, and go down before the rain stops you."' Now it happened in the meantime that the sky became black with clouds and wind, and there was a heavy rain. So Ahab rode away and went to Jezreel. Then the hand of the LORD came upon Elijah; and he girded up his loins and ran ahead of Ahab to the entrance of Jezreel" (I Kings 18:41-46).

Samuel
"And Samuel said, 'Gather all Israel to Mizpah, and I will pray to the Lord for you.'" (I Samuel 7:5).

Moses
"Then Moses pleaded with the Lord his God, and said: 'Lord, why does Your wrath burn hot against Your people whom You have brought out of the land of Egypt with great power and with a mighty hand? Why should the Egyptians speak and say, "He brought them out to harm them, to kill them in the mountains, and to consume them from the face of the earth?" Turn from Your fierce wrath, and relent from this harm to Your people. Remember Abraham, Isaac and Israel, Your servants, to whom You swore by Your own self, and said to them, "I will multiply your descendants as the stars of heaven; and all this land that I have spoken of I give to your descendants, and they shall inherit it forever."' So the Lord relented from the harm which He said He would do to His people" (Exodus 32:11-14). (See Exodus 15:25, 32:30-34.)

Old Testament Prophets
"But if they are prophets, and if the word of the Lord is with them, let them now make intercession to the Lord of hosts, that the vessels which are left in the house of the Lord, in the house of the king of Judah, and at Jerusalem, do not go to Babylon" (Jeremiah 27:18). (See Jeremiah 36:25.)

Daniel
"Now while I was speaking, praying, and confessing my sin and the sin of my people Israel, and presenting my supplication before the Lord my God for the holy mountain of my God . . ." (Daniel 9:20). (See Daniel 9:10, 23.)

King David

"Then David lifted his eyes and saw the angel of the Lord standing between earth and heaven, having in his hand a drawn sword stretched out over Jerusalem. So David and the elders, clothed in sackcloth, fell on their faces" (I Chronicles 21:16).

Job

"And the Lord restored Job's losses when he prayed for his friends. Indeed the Lord gave Job twice as much as he had before" (Job 42:10).

Apostle Paul

"For this reason I bow my knees to the Father of our Lord Jesus Christ" (Ephesians 3:14).

Jesus

"Therefore He is also able to save to the uttermost those who come to God through Him, since He always lives to make intercession for them" (Hebrews 7:25). (See Luke 23:34; Isaiah 53:12.)

Finally, You!

Within our nation are several million potential prayer-intercessors. Let us arise and stand in the gap for our nation. First, let us repent and find cleansing and healing. Then, let us intercede for our national, spiritual state. Let us repent of our wickedness, perversion, idolatry, witchcraft, occultism, immorality, injustice, racism, abortion, hate crimes and homosexuality.

In responding to the broken heart of God, we need to identify with the sins of the nation in personal and corporate repentance. God's desire is to show His gracious loving-kindness toward the nations. (See Matthew 20:31-32; Isaiah 49:6.)

"Therefore the Lord will wait, that He may be gracious to you; and therefore He will be exalted, that He may have mercy on you. For the Lord is a God of justice; blessed are all those who wait for Him. For the people shall dwell in Zion at Jerusalem; you shall weep no more. He will be very gracious to you at the sound of your cry; when He hears it, He will answer you" (Isaiah 30:18-19).

Further Study

1. Read Ezekiel 22:30,31. What does this passage teach concerning God's priority for Christians? What is God searching for?

2. What is the impact of neglecting intercessory prayer?

3. How and why is it easy for Christians to neglect intercession?

4. Who are some of the great "gap standing" intercessors in the Bible and what can we learn from their prayer ministry?

Notes

1.   Gospel Herald.
2.   E.M. Bounds.
3.   John Wesley.

The Strategy
Components for Effective Intercession

Chapter Ten:
Gap Standing, Hedge Building, & Cup Filling

In their one hundred-year prayer movement, which began in 1727, the Moravians proved a living portrait of gap standing, hedge building and cup filling. For one hundred years, twenty-four hours a day, seven days a week, fifty-two weeks a year, they sent up prayers before God. The Moravians' new light on essential biblical truths influenced John and Charles Wesley, preparing them for the revival that swept England and reached America. The Wesleyan revivals broke out because someone had been unceasingly gap standing, hedge building and cup filling for over one hundred years.

The missionary enterprise in America originated from the famous "Haystack Prayer Meeting" at Williams College in Massachusetts in 1811. As a group of students met in a field for prayer, a storm arose. Taking refuge under a haystack, they continued their prayer meeting, consecrating their lives to work for Christ in the heathen world.

Everything that fulfills the gospel seems to start in prayer. Someone, some group whom God is stirring, stands in the gap and builds a hedge.

Gap Standing

The word "gap" in the Hebrew means a rupture or breach. This word is taken from a military context, and applies to besiegers who rush into a city through breaches in the wall. The besieging army would attack one specific place in the wall until it was weakened. Then with united strength, the enemy would rush the wall, causing a breach or break.

The gap standing soldier's responsibility was to risk his life by standing in the breach and single-handedly repelling the enemy. This was known to be one of the bravest acts of a soldier, since he risked severe injury and danger. Often these soldiers gave their lives to fill the gap and save the city. A gap standing soldier was a highly respected and sought out name among the soldiers.

Principles of Gap Standing

The principle of gap standing, as applied to intercessory prayer, comes from God Himself in Ezekiel 22:30. The whole Church is responsible to stand in the gap for cities and the nations of the world. The power of one person standing in the gap is established in Scripture. It is a fact that one gap standing person can save a city, a people, a nation. The difference that one person, one church or group of praying gap standers can make should motivate every Christian to learn how to stand in the gap.

Moses models the power of a single gap stander in a crisis. (See Psalm 106:23; Exodus 32:30-34.)

"Then Moses pleaded with the Lord his God, and said: 'Lord, why does Your wrath burn hot against Your people whom You have brought out of the land of Egypt with great power and with a mighty hand? Why should the Egyptians speak, and say, "He brought them out to harm them, to kill them in the mountains, and to consume them from the face of the earth?" Turn from Your fierce wrath, and relent from this harm to Your people. Remember Abraham, Isaac, and Israel, Your servants, to whom You swore by Your own self, and said to them, "I will multiply your descendants as the stars of heaven; and all this land that I have spoken of I give to your descendants, and they shall inherit it forever." So the Lord relented from the harm which He said He would do to His people' " (Exodus 32:11-14).

The Power of Gap Standing

The power of gap standing prayer is captured in a frequently discussed phrase found in Exodus 32:14.

"So the Lord repented from the harm which He said He would do to His people" (Exodus 32:14).

This example of God's repentance can be explained by understanding the concept of anthropomorphism. Anthropomorphism is a description of God in human form. This verse shows that God can and does change

His intentions and emotions toward men when given proper grounds for doing so. He does not change His basic character or God-attributes.

The terms "repented," "relented" or "the changing of the mind" are used thirty-eight times in the Old Testament. God's activity is explained through anthropomorphism. In strictly human terms, God embarked on a different course of action from that which had already been suggested as a possibility, owing to some new factor that is usually conditioned on man's response. We are not to see Moses, or man, altering God's purpose toward Israel by His anger, but we are to see him carrying out of God's purposes through intercessory prayer that aligns with God and His desired will.

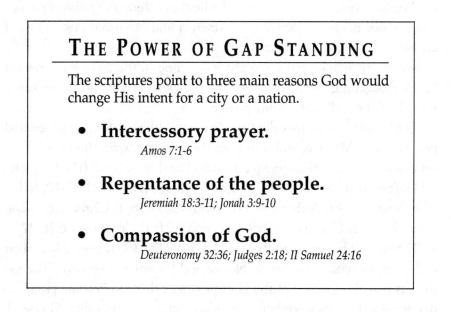

THE POWER OF GAP STANDING

The scriptures point to three main reasons God would change His intent for a city or a nation.

- ## Intercessory prayer.
  Amos 7:1-6

- ## Repentance of the people.
  Jeremiah 18:3-11; Jonah 3:9-10

- ## Compassion of God.
  Deuteronomy 32:36; Judges 2:18; II Samuel 24:16

The intercessory prayer of Moses was an appeal to God to be consistent with His nature, a declaration of confidence in His love. The intercessory prayer of Moses was to plead with God to turn from His wrath and reveal His mercy.

Gap standing prayer proves the force of one pray-er. God's people have the unique privilege of being able to pray for mercy when judgment is deserved and for the supernatural intervention of God when human resources are useless.

In Genesis 18:25-27, Abraham stands in the gap for a city and again God reveals His desire to redeem, heal and save instead of destroy. Abraham moves into the breach to call on the merciful nature of God, and God's response is "Yes! Yes, I will save this city based on Abraham's gap standing, if I could find even ten repentant people." This certainly provides a sense of hope for every gap standing believer.

The Time to Stand in the Gap

" 'So I sought for a man among them who would make a wall, and stand in the gap before Me on behalf of the land, that I should not destroy it; but I found no one' " (Ezekiel 22:30).

Now is the time to answer God's call to the Church to stand in the gap for a nation. This is a high calling, and a calling that some will not heed for many different reasons–ignorance, selfishness, hard heartedness, smallness of soul, or just believing the lie that intercessory prayer cannot and has not made a difference in America and other nations. This, of course, is not biblical thinking.

Let us first ponder Scripture about standing in the gap for the nation before proceeding any further. A call to prayer, humility and repentance is God's call for all interceding people.

"If My people who are called by My name will humble themselves, and pray and seek My face, and turn from their wicked ways, then I will hear from heaven, and will forgive their sin and heal their land" (II Chronicles 7:14). (See also Ezekiel 22:30; Exodus 32:13-14; Jeremiah 18:7-10; Isaiah 55:6; Jeremiah 9:1; Nehemiah 1:6; I Kings 8:35-36; II Chronicles 4:2-4; Psalm 71:18; II Chronicles 16:9; Jeremiah 8:21; II Chronicles 6:26-27.)

Throughout history, Scripture testifies that when God's people kept their end of the covenant, they were blessed and blessed and blessed. The sad story is that the blessing of the Lord provoked them to become proud, to develop sinful habits, to embrace new idols and to turn away from God–and, most of the time, this all took place within one generation. Today, with great sadness, we witness the decline of our nation, the disappearance of godly virtues, and an abandonment of our godly heritage. Our only hope is a true Christian revival of religion, a revival of the true Church, a revival birthed in true repentance.

For thirteen months Evan Roberts prayed for revival to come to Wales. David Matthews, who was present at the Welsh Revival of 1904 said this of Evan Roberts, "Prayer was the keynote of his tireless life. No action taken or entered into was done so without definitely committing the matter to God. His soul appeared to be saturated through with the spirit of prayer. It was the atmosphere in which he moved and lived. Whenever one looked on his face, he seemed engaged in intercession."[1]

We are, once again, calling our nation to a day of repentance. The *Promise Keepers* hosted a "Sacred Assembly" of men in Washington, D.C., for a "Standing in the Gap" prayer and repentance day. More than one million men traveled to our capitol, and countless others participated from their home base. This is a day of calling out to God for mercy. This is the spirit of intercession.

The Old Testament records at least twelve times when Israel gathered together for one or more days of prayer, fasting, confession and repentance of sin. Concerning the "Standing in the Gap" day of prayer, *Promise Keepers* state their purpose as follows: "We will gather to confess our poverty of spirit, humbly naming our personal and collective sins, pleading for God's mercy, and preparing our hearts for the revival and spiritual awakening God wishes to send."[2]

Gap standing is our job description as prayer-intercessors! Our nation, and, obviously, any nation that will respond to God with prayer and fasting, has the potential to receive a true outpouring of the Holy Spirit.

Hedge Building

A broken-down hedge allows spiritual fruit to be ruined.

The word "hedge" means "to surround with a fence or a wall, to protect, to set anyone who is in trouble, distress or danger in a safe place, to keep out the enemies of the vineyard, the flock, the house or the city." Intercessory prayer involves the ability to build spiritual walls or hedges around people, houses, marriages, children, churches, cities and regions. This is the Nehemiah 4:7-8 principle: rebuilding the walls of the city to provide protection from the attacking enemies. The Sanballats and Tobiahs seek out the gaps in the wall, which provide avenues for the enemy to enter the city. Intercessory prayer closes those gaps and rebuilds the walls.

A Broken Down Hedge Allows Spiritual Destruction

- A broken-down hedge allows continual satanic harassment in and around those areas that especially need spiritual protection. "He who digs a pit will fall into it, and whoever breaks through a wall will be bitten by a serpent" (Ecclesiastes 10:8).

- A broken-down hedge allows God's vineyard to be trampled by demonic powers.

  "And now, please let Me tell you what I will do to My vineyard: I will take away its hedge, and it shall be burned; and break down its wall, and it shall be trampled down" (Isaiah 5:5).

- A broken-down hedge allows spiritual fruit, the labor and sacrifice of God's people, to be ruined. "Why have You broken down her hedges, so that all who pass by the way pluck her fruit?" (Psalm 80:12).

- A broken-down hedge allows for specific seats of Satan to be established. A seat of Satan may be a geographic location that is highly oppressed and demonically controlled by a certain dark principality. From this seat the enemy conducts warfare on a specific area of the city. This seat of Satan must be destroyed through a strategic level of prayer warfare. "I know your works, and where you dwell, where Satan's throne is. And you hold fast to My name, and did not deny My faith even in the days in which Antipas was My faithful martyr, who was killed among you, where Satan dwells" (Revelation 2:13).

  "You have broken down all his hedges; you have brought his strongholds to ruin" (Psalm 89:40).

PORTLAND–AN EXAMPLE OF BROKEN-DOWN HEDGES

Let me illustrate this by using my own city, Portland, Oregon. Our region has broken-down hedges, as seen in the demonic social and spiritual problems.

- Portland is a major drug distribution center in our nation. "Portland's Pacific Rim location, access to a major waterway and its strategic position in the middle of the West Coast drug pipeline are all factors that contribute to a volume of drug trafficking activity beyond that usually associated with a medium sized city." (Multnomah County Alcohol and Drug Program)

- Portland ranks fifth among metropolitan areas surveyed (behind Manhattan, San Diego, Philadelphia, and Chicago) in drug use and drug-related crimes.

- Portland is first in the nation for marijuana use and methamphetamine use.

- Portland is a hotbed of pornography and sexual vice, with more topless bars per capita than any other United States city. From 1989 to 1993 the number of strip clubs in Portland increased from 18 to 54, an increase of 300%.

- Portland's overall world view is humanistic. Humanism is the belief that the universe consists only of what can be verified through scientific investigation or objective reason. The humanist and the New Age movements are a strong influence in the Northwest.

- Portland has at least 93 New Age centers and places of New Age information. New Age is clearly connected to witchcraft and Satanism, inviting spirit guides to operate. They work as power boosters to the territorial spirits that dwell over geographic regions. demonic activity in our city, our public education systems. and our various

The Church of Portland has a spiritual responsibility to rebuild the spiritual hedges that will protect our region from seats of Satan. This rebuilding of the hedge is accomplished though a call to repentance, unifying the churches, and establishing strategic level intercessory prayer in every local church, and unified corporate prayer with all the churches. Satan seeks to drive a wedge between the Church and the city, creating an "us against them" mentality. The Church often views city government as its enemy and the city often views the Church in a negative light. This stronghold is demolished when the churches learn to bless the city, pray for the city and serve the city.

To build hedges we must see the broken-down areas and repair them. The Holy Spirit is both the Envisioner and the Enabler. As the Envisioner, the Holy Spirit shows us with spiritual eyes what God is doing. As the Enabler, the Holy Spirit gives us the power to bring the vision to pass.

Filling the Prayer Cup

Not only are we, as the church, to stand in the gap and, rebuild the hedge, but we are also to fill the prayer cup.

" 'Therefore I have poured out My indignation on them; I have consumed them with the fire of My wrath; and I have recompensed their deeds on their own heads,' says the Lord God" (Ezekiel 22:31).

Intercessory prayer has the power to hold back destruction upon the land and to bring healing instead. God will pour out from one of two cups referred to in Scripture: the cup filled with the prayers of the saints, or the cup filled with the iniquity of the people.

The cup of iniquity is referred to in Psalm 75:8, as one translation reads: "Within the Lord's dispensing power of a cup of destiny with fermenting wine, well mixed."[4] The cup of fermenting wine represents the collective generational sins and the iniquity of any given nation or people group. When the cup is full, the wrath of God will be poured out. (See Habakkuk 2:16; Revelation 14:10, 16:19, 17:4, 18:6.)

Our responsibility is to fill the cup of prayers so that God will pour out His Spirit of mercy, not wrath; revival, not judgment; healing, not destruction. (See Psalm 141:2, 5:8; Luke 1:9-11; Revelation 5:8; II Chronicles 7:14.)

"Then another angel, having a golden censer, came and stood at the altar. And he was given much incense, that he should offer it with the prayers of all the saints upon the golden altar which was before the throne. And the smoke of the incense, with the prayers of the saints, ascended before God from the angel's hand" (Revelation 8:3-4).

This happened in our church as united prayer-intercession turned a crisis into a victory. The call went out to the church one August morning that one of our elder's wives, who had been ill all week, had lapsed into a coma that morning. Doctors called in specialists to determine what was causing her illness. Approximately 200 people gathered at the church that night for prayer-intercession. After about an hour, the group was officially dismissed and those who were still burdened to continue praying were invited to remain. Nearly twenty people continued in deep intercession until around midnight. As there was a release of the burden, the warfare died down, and the sound of praise began to be heard.

Later, the intercessors were told that it was around midnight that the doctors found the virus they were fighting and began administering the proper medication. By the next morning, this woman was awake and on the mend. The call to prayer had gone forth all over the world for this woman. It is estimated that hundreds of prayers went up for her over a twelve-hour period. Truly the cup of intercession was rapidly filled to bring the full release of her healing.

Gap standing, hedge building and cup filling are the call of the Spirit, now, for the nations of the world. In addition to gap standing, hedge building, and cup filling there are many different aspects to intercessory prayer. In the following chapters we will develop five "goals" which included the following: interceding with spiritual travail, striking the target, obtaining supernatural assistance, setting divine boundary lines, and eliminating the enemy. This is not to limit the goals of intercessory prayer to a mere five, but I have narrowed the overall view of intercessory prayer to include, at least, these first five primary ones. Right now, God desires to pour out revival, restoration and healing upon our land. Let us strive toward these goals and respond by saying, "Here I am; send me. Here am I, Lord; use me to stand in the gap for my city and my nation."

GOALS OF INTERCESSORY PRAYER
- Interceding with Spiritual Travail
- Striking the Target
- Obtaining Supernatural Assistance
- Setting Divine Boundary Lines
- Eliminating the Enemy

Further Study

1. Define and describe gap standing, hedge building, and cup filling.

2. What is the power of gap standing? What can it accomplish?

3. What are the results of a broken down hedge? Do you see any evidences of broken hedges in your church, family, or community? If so, what are they?

4. How can the rebuilding of spiritual hedges be accomplished?

5. Why is it important to fill the prayer cup? What is the result of failing to do so?

Notes

1.   David Matthews, I Saw the Welsh Revival, 41.

2.   "Standing in the Gap" Brochure, (Promise Keepers, 1997).

Chapter Eleven:
Interceeding with Spiritual Travail

One Sunday night in April of 1912, an American woman was very weary, yet she could not sleep because of an oppression of fear. At last she felt a burden of prayer and with tremendous, earnest travail began to pray for her husband, who was then in the mid-Atlantic, homeward bound on the Titanic. As the hours went by, she could get no assurance and kept praying in agony until about five o'clock in the morning, when a great peace possessed her and she slept. Meanwhile, her husband, Col. Gracie, was among the doomed hundreds who were frantically trying to launch the lifeboats from the great ship, its vitals torn out by an iceberg. He had himself given up all hope of being saved and was doing his best to help the women and children. He wished he could get a last message through to his wife and cried from his heart, "Good-bye, my darling!" Then, as the ship plunged to her watery grave, he was sucked down in the giant whirlpool. Instinctively he began to swim underwater, ice cold as it was, crying in his heart. Suddenly he came to the surface and found himself near an overturned lifeboat. Along with several others he climbed aboard and was picked up by another lifeboat at about five o'clock in the morning, the very time that the peace came to his wife's prayer life.

Oh, that we could travail in supplication and intercession in order to see supernatural results! The desire of the Holy Spirit is to motivate entire congregations into a deeper level of prayer-intercession, in order to release the supernatural powers of God in an obvious and awesome manner, resulting in an awesome harvest of souls.

The Holy Spirit is nurturing the Church into a deeper relationship with Jesus, the Great Intercessor. Intercessory prayer is an expression of relationship that is founded on covenant and exercised by faith and patience.

Intercessory prayer is an intervention, petition or treaty on behalf of another person. This kind of prayer breaks through whatever obstacles it must, until the answer comes from God. All intercession is real and serious communication with God. It is not casual, even when beautifully simple. It is sacred; it is important to God; it is a Kingdom action. It is at times a spiritual labor and an intense spiritual effort.

"May God open our eyes to see what the holy ministry of intercession is, to which, as His royal priesthood, we have been set apart. May He give us a large and strong heart to believe what mighty influence our prayers can exert. May all fear as to our being able to fulfill our vocation vanish as we see Jesus living ever to pray, living in us to pray, and standing surety for our prayer life" (Andrew Murray).[1]

Spiritual Travail

Spiritual travail is a level of intensity marked by a Holy Spirit burden to actually bring to pass, through prayer, a given promise, a prophetic insight, or a Holy Spirit illuminated need in a person, church, city or nation.

Samuel Chadwick, a great commentator of the past, stated, "There is marked absence of travail. There is much phrasing, but little pleading. Prayer has become a form of poetry, instead of passion. The powerlessness of the Church needs no other explanation; to be prayerless is to be both passionless and powerless."[2]

Revival is birthed out of the womb of intercession...

The Holy Spirit seizes us with a Holy Spirit burden, a strong anointing for Holy Spirit intercession that becomes a birthing process in the spirit realm. Revival is birthed out of the womb of intercession, that is, God seizing people and birthing His purposes through intercession. This kind of intercessory prayer requires spiritual travail.

Every woman, who has given birth to a child, understands the meaning the word "travail." Men can use the word but, obviously, without the intense experience and deep knowledge of what this word actually means. When a woman has experienced the travail of bringing forth a child, she only needs to hear someone speaking this word to remember her own experiences, pain, time and energy exerted to birth a child.

When the Bible speaks of travail in connection with intercession, we begin to understand what is involved. One of Martin Luther's friends described the great reformer in the act of prayer this way: "His prayer become a storm, a wrestling with God, the power, greatness and holy simplicity which it is difficult to compare with any other human emotion."[3]

Hebrew Meaning of "Travail"

The Hebrew words for "travail" give colorful meaning to this subject. The Hebrew word *yalad* means "to give birth to something, a time of delivery or intense labor." The word *telah* means "to be in a state of distress, trouble and agitation."

"Before she was in labor, she gave birth; before her pain came, she delivered a male child. Who has heard such a thing? Who has seen such things? Shall the earth be made to give birth in one day? Or shall a nation be born at once? For as soon as Zion was in labor, she gave birth to her children" (Isaiah 66:7-8).

Here we have two uses of the Hebrew word "travail," which involves an intense labor to bring something forth.

"Then they journeyed from Bethel. And when there was but a little distance to go to Ephrath, Rachel labored in childbirth, and she had hard labor" (Genesis 35:16).

The word "travail" means to force something through labor, to bring it out. On the negative side, this can be a grievous, unfulfilling drudgery, causing frustration, sorrow and weariness. But on the positive side, laboring can result in bringing forth a vision or the purpose of God, which is not grievous, but fulfilling and satisfying to the Spirit.

Greek Meaning of "Travail"

The Greek words *tikto*, *odino* and *mochthos* are translated "travail" in the New Testament. These words mean "to bear, to bring forth, to be delivered, to produce, to feel the pains of childbirth, to labor in something, to toil." These words could also mean "a time of sadness because of the pain." This word again describes the process of birthing in the spirit realm that which God has desired to bring forth.

"My little children, for whom I labor in birth again until Christ is formed in you" (Galatians 4:19).

"For you remember, brethren, our labor and toil; for laboring night and day, that we might not be a burden to any of you, we preached to you the gospel of God" (I Thessalonians 2:9). (See I Thessalonians 5:3; II Thessalonians 3:8.)

"Likewise the Spirit also helps in our weaknesses. For we do not know what we should pray for as we ought, but the Spirit Himself makes intercession for us with groanings which cannot be uttered" (Romans 8:26).

Travail and the Holy Spirit

Spiritual travail and intercessory prayer, together, produce the desired results of the Holy Spirit. As we begin to give ourselves to travail, we will feel the burden of something so deeply in our hearts, souls and emotions that we actually feel physical pain. As we carry the burden for a soul, a city, or a nation, there can be times of spiritual travail. Spiritual travail can be a seasonal activity of the Holy Spirit, as the Holy Spirit visits intercessors to bring them to their knees, to wrestle and to intercede for a specific need.

Spiritual travail is not something that a person can conjure up himself or can learn just by reading a book about it. Spiritual travail must be given by the Holy Spirit and learned in the school of the Spirit. Those people, who are involved with intercessory prayer as a lifestyle, are people who have experienced spiritual travail, labor and birthing pains. It could be that they are interceding about a promise that has been given, or interceding for the healing of someone's body or the saving of a person's soul. This travail can last for minutes; it can last for several hours; or it can go on for several weeks or months. People are seized by spiritual travail that will cause them to feel such pain and burden for the situation that they will call on the name of the Lord and stand in the gap in that crucial moment.

Travail and Prophetic Intercession

Whenever God gives a church, or an individual, prophetic words—that is, quickened words or words of the future—these prophetic declarations are only part of God's will and work. Prophetic declaration must be followed up with prophetic intercession that births what God has said. Intercession brings the promise to fulfillment. (See II Chronicles 6:4; Psalm 105:19; Romans 4:20.)

"This charge I commit to you, son Timothy, according to the prophecies previously made concerning you, that by them you may wage the good warfare, having faith and a good conscience, which some having rejected, concerning the faith have suffered shipwreck" (I Timothy 1:18-19).

Travail and Tears

As we move into travail-intercession, not only do we claim our prophetic declarations, but we also, at times, are moved to pray with deep feeling and emotion, even to tears. Tears are a sign of

Tears are simply a liquidating of our true selves.

something breaking up inside of us and freeing our emotions. Tears are a cleansing agent to the soul and spirit. The Bible has a theology of tears. Tears are literal reflections of our inner persons, pieces of our memories, our hurts, our experiences. Tears are simply a liquidating of our true selves. (See Psalms 42:3, 56:8, 126:5; Acts 20:19; II Kings 20:5.)

An elderly missionary to Nigeria was agonizing over her return to the United States. Although she knew she had to return, her heart was broken over the people she was leaving and the many villages yet to be reached. As her heart cried for the nation of Nigeria, her tears formed a pool in front of her and she asked, "God, store up my tears in a bottle and for every tear let one soul be saved." As she travailed for a nation, her passion for the lost souls poured out in tears.

In the book of Lamentations, which is a book of intercession, the prophet states, "My eyes fail with tears, my heart is troubled; my bile is poured on the ground because of the destruction of the daughter of my people, because the children and the infants faint in the streets of the city. . . . Their heart cried out to the Lord, 'O wall of the daughter of Zion, let tears run down like a river day and night; give yourself no relief; give your eyes no rest. Arise, cry out in the night, at the beginning of the watches; pour out your heart like water before the face of the Lord. Lift your hands toward Him for the life of your young children, who faint from hunger at the head of every street.' " (Lamentations 2:11, 3:18-19).

Intercession is made with strong feeling, deep emotions. The Bible speaks of our tears of intercession as being bottled up and kept by the Lord. When we pour out our hearts before the Lord with strong, spiritual travail, there will be times of much weeping and free flowing tears. (See Hebrews 5:7.)

"Therefore watch, and remember that for three years I did not cease to warn everyone night and day with tears" (Acts 20:31).

Supplication and intercession, the prayer that will not take "no" for an answer, that storms the battlements of heaven and brings confusion and defeat to all the powers of hell, even death itself. That is true spiritual travail.

Further Study

1. What does it mean to intercede with spiritual travail?

2. What role does the Holy Spirit play in intercession with spiritual travail?

3. What do tears signify in the Bible? What role do they play in travail intercession?

Notes

1.   Andrew Murray, <u>With Christ in the School of Prayer</u>.

2.   Samuel Chadwick.

3.   Martin Luther.

Chapter Twelve:
Striking the Target with Supernatural Assistance

In Frank Peretti's book, *This Present Darkness*, a brief passage describes interceding by striking the target:

> The night scene of the quiet street was a collage of stark blue moonlight and bottomless shadows, but one shadow did not stir with the wind as did the tree shadows. It crawled, quivered, moved along the street toward the church while any light it crossed seemed to sink into blackness as if it were a breach torn into space. But this shadow had a creature-like shape and, as it neared the church, the scratching of claws on the ground, the faint rustling of breeze blown, membranous wings wafting just above the creature's shoulders. It had arms and it had legs but it seemed to move without them, crossing the street and mounting the front steps of the church. Its leering, bulbous eyes reflected the stark blue light face of the full moon with their own jaundiced glow. The gnarled head protruded from hunched shoulders and wisps of rancid breath seethed and labored hisses through rows of jagged fangs. It either laughed or coughed. The wheezes puffing out from deep within its throat could have been either. From its crawling posture it reared up on its legs and looked about the quiet neighborhood, the black, leathery jowls pulling back into a hideous, death-mask grin. It moved toward the front door. The black hand passed through the door like a spear through liquid. The body hobbled forward and penetrated the door, but only halfway.

Suddenly, as if colliding with a speeding wall, the creature was knocked backward into a raging tumble down the steps, the glowing red breath tracing a corkscrew trail through the air. With an eerie cry of rage and indignation, it gathered itself off the sidewalk and stared at the strange door that would not let it pass through. The creature screamed and covered its eyes, then felt itself being grabbed by a huge, powerful vise of a hand. In an instant it was hurling through space like a rag doll, outside again, forcefully ousted. The wings hummed in a blur as it banked sharply in a flying turn and headed for the door again, red vapors chugging in dashes and streaks from its nostrils, its talons bared and poised for attack, a ghostly siren of a scream rising in its throat. Like an arrow through a target, like a bullet through a board, it streaked through the door. There was an explosion of suffocating vapor, one final scream and the flailing of withering arms and legs, then there was nothing at all except the ebbing stench of sulfur. Two visitors which were angels looked inside of the church. "Let's see the man of God." As they passed the pews and the worn carpeted platform, he said, "This is the one. Even now he's interceding, standing before the Lord for the sake of the people, for the town. Almost every night he's here, but he's the only one. He's alone."[1]

Intercessory prayer is the spear that focuses with authority on the desired circumstance, event, person or nation, with strategic targeting. To strike the target requires specific intercessory prayer.

Intercessory prayer must involve a specific target.

"Then the Lord said to Joshua, 'Stretch out the spear that is in your hand toward Ai, for I will give it into your hand.' And Joshua stretched out the spear that was in his hand toward the city" (Joshua 8:18).

"Until now you have asked nothing in My name. Ask, and you will receive, that your joy may be full" (John 16:24).

Striking the Target

Intercessory prayer must involve a specific target. Spiritual enemies and circumstances that must be broken through often block the target. At times the target needs to be struck with force. The force of intercession is one of the greatest weapons known to the Christian.

Our young adults group experiences target intercession through prayer walks around the building at which they meet in downtown Portland. Each week they walk around the park, praying for the people there, binding the works of the enemy, blessing those they see. One day a young man stopped the prayer team and asked them, "What are you doing here? You're up to something. I can tell. Things have changed since you started coming around here. Who are you?"

After hearing that they were praying, he explained, "I always used to come here to do drugs and to sell drugs. Lately, I can't do that anymore. For one thing, no one wants to buy from me here. And every time I come to do drugs, I begin to realize what a mess my life is and how miserable I am. I begin to think about God and what my life is about. That doesn't happen to me when I do drugs anywhere else. Why does it happen here?" A police officer later confirmed that drugs were no longer being sold in that area because the dealers had moved elsewhere.

"But lift up your rod, and stretch out your hand over the sea and divide it. And the children of Israel shall go on dry ground through the midst of the sea" (Exodus 14:16).

Spiritual intercession has the force of dividing or breaking through that which hinders the prayer from being answered. The word "divide" in the Hebrew means "a strenuous cleaving, resulting in a bursting forth." To divide means "to strike with great force so as to bring a breakthrough" or "to cause an opening where before it was shut." It is the forcefulness that causes something to split open.

Intercessory prayer involves specific spiritual warfare over people's lives, over circumstances, cities and churches. It is with this warfare that we force through or split open that which has been bound by the spirit realm. A spiritual victory is brought about by strategic intercessory prayer. Long-standing obstacles are removed, releasing the person prayed for into a new dimension. This is striking the target.

Let me share one very specific illustration of striking the target through corporate intercession. In March of 1996, I began teaching on general prayer and prayer-intercession at our church. For the next year and a half we preached, taught and practiced prayer. As a church, we prayed and interceded for our church, our city and the harvest.

In July 1997, we experienced a unique and powerful spiritual breakthrough during a conference we were having at the church. Ken Gott, from England, spoke on "The Shout that Stopped God." During this conference God had spoken some specific challenges and promises to the churches of Portland about His heart for our city and His desire to move in our city. As the message drew to a close, the congregation stood and began to intercede for a breakthrough. God had stated His will for our city, and we wanted to see it fulfilled. For twenty-five

For twenty-five minutes 3,000 people raised their voice in a shout.

minutes three thousand people raised their voices in a prolonged shout of intercession. Something seemed to snap in the spirit realm at that moment in time, marking the dethroning of ungodly spiritual authorities in our city. A breakthrough for harvest was then possible.

This is not the only time our church or other churches praying in the city have experienced definite spiritual breakthrough, but it was another blow to the kingdom of darkness. We had invaded enemy territory once again.

"So David went to Baal Perazim, and David defeated them there; and he said, 'The Lord has broken through my enemies before me, like a breakthrough of water.' Therefore he called the name of that place Baal Perazim" (II Samuel 5:20).

Striking the Target of a Specific Crisis

Intercessory prayer strikes the target when there is a specific crisis at hand. "Peter was therefore kept in prison, but constant prayer was offered to God for him by the church" (Acts 12:5).

Today, many people, who need constant intercession, are kept in spiritual prisons. We must strike the target, shatter the bondages and remove the long-standing obstacles to allow them to be free in the Spirit. We need to ask specifically when we pray for intercessory targets and have faith to believe that our target will be struck. With intercessory prayer, we need to stretch our spirits out–as Joshua did toward Ai–toward every situation when we have faith to move. Striking the target involves petitioning, asking specifically in faith without wavering, knowing that God has given us the authority to pray in this manner.

"And the king said to Queen Esther, 'The Jews have killed and destroyed five hundred men in Shushan the citadel, and the ten sons of Haman. What have they done in the rest of the king's provinces? Now what is your petition? It shall be granted to you. Or what is your further request? It shall be done.' Then Esther said, 'If it pleases the king, let it be granted to the Jews who are in Shushan to do again tomorrow according to today's decree, and let Haman's ten sons be hanged on the gallows.' So the king commanded this to be done; the decree was issued in Shushan, and they hanged Haman's ten sons" (Esther 9:12-14).

This is specific-targeting, intercessory prayer. If the Holy Spirit were to ask you, "What is your petition? What is your heart's desire?" what would you ask for? Is your heart aligned with scriptural truth and biblical affections?

In Mark 10:46-52 we have the account of another person who prayed to Jesus by asking specifically. "Now they came to Jericho. As He went out of Jericho with His disciples and a great multitude, blind Bartimaeus, the son of Timaeus, sat by the road begging. And when he heard that it was Jesus of Nazareth, he began to cry out and say, 'Jesus, Son of David, have mercy on me!' Then many warned him to be quiet; but he cried out all the more, 'Son of David, have mercy on me!' So Jesus stood still and commanded him to be called. Then they called the blind man, saying to him, 'Be of good cheer. Rise, He is calling you.' And throwing aside his garment, he rose and came to Jesus. So Jesus answered and said to him, 'What do you want Me to do for you?' The blind man said to Him, 'Rabboni, that I may receive my sight.' Then Jesus said to him, 'Go your way; your faith has made you well.' And immediately he received his sight and followed Jesus on the road."

The question Jesus asked this man could be asked of every intercessor: "What do you want me to do for you?" At this point, we need to be specific. "Lord, I need you to save this person I have been praying for." Or "Lord, this person needs healing, and I am interceding and standing in the gap for him." Or "Lord, this business is going through a crisis, and I am asking You to do such and such for it." "Lord, I want to be specific. I would like my faith to be fulfilled in the answer to this prayer."

And the Scripture says, "immediately he received what he asked." The Lord does want us to receive what we specifically ask for.

Supernatural Assistance

Intercessory prayer is needed to release healing to society's troubled waters–throughout Scripture, waters of the sea are used to describe masses of humanity. Moses' intercession led him to cast a tree into the bitter waters. This is descriptive of our purpose as we release healing through intercessory prayer.

"So he cried out to the Lord, and the Lord showed him a tree. When he cast it into the waters, the waters were made sweet. There He made a statute and an ordinance for them. And there He tested them" (Exodus 15:25).

Today's society is being destroyed by sin. We, as intercessors, need to begin to plead with the Lord to cast a tree into the waters of our nation, into the waters of our city, into the waters of our neighborhoods and into the waters of our homes. The waters are bitter, but the tree cast in can make the waters sweet.

The tree that we are speaking about is the cross. The power of the resurrection of the Lord Jesus Christ, the power of the gospel, the power of the cross, has sacred power to sweeten the bitter waters of our society. God's answer for the troubled waters is the foolishness of the Christ message.

"And I, brethren, when I came to you, did not come with excellence of speech or of wisdom declaring to you the testimony of God. For I determined not to know anything among you except Jesus Christ and Him crucified. I was with you in weakness, in fear, and in much trembling. And my speech and my preaching were not with persuasive words of human wisdom, but in demonstration of the Spirit and of power" (I Corinthians 2:1-4).

Intercessory prayer releases supernatural blessing into every bitter part of our culture.

As Moses heard the cry of Israel because the waters were bitter at Marah, so we hear the cry of our society. (See Exodus 15:22-26.) The water is polluted, rancid and bitter. Only the cross will transform the waters.

The water looked fine, but it was bitter. Many things in this life look good, but experience proves them bitter. We cannot judge earthly things according to their appearances. We are often disappointed in life's temptations because things are not always as good as they appear. Houses, businesses, friendships, possessions–many of the things we long for prove to be disappointing.

Marah represents that which looks good but is actually bitter. Marah represents the trials and disappointments of life that lead many to murmur rather than to pray, to become bitter rather than to rejoice. Even the apparent trivial things of life can cause bitter disappointment, and there are many people living in Marah, many businesses in Marah, many marriages in Marah. Many have experienced the bitter waters of life.

Intercessory prayer releases supernatural blessing into these bitter waters, releases the sweetness of Jesus into every bitter part of our culture. As intercessors release the tree, bitter waters become sweet. Intercessory prayer can cause bitter people to begin to look to the source of healing, that is, the tree or the cross. Only through intercession will these people be reached. Many who have tasted the bitterness of life are closed, hurt, disillusioned, blind, and they will not call upon the name of the Lord. They do not know the Scripture that says, "I Am the Lord that healeth thee. I Am your doctor. I Am your answer. I Am the sweetness for your life." But through intercessory prayer, the way is opened up for the tree to be cast into the waters of these bitter lives.

Intercessory prayer opens the eyes of all who fear the odds that they face in life, in marriage, in business or in ministry. Intercessory prayer opens the eyes of the young servants, so they can see the supernatural assistance available to them.

"And when the servant of the man of God arose early and went out, there was an army, surrounding the city with horses and chariots. And his servant said to him, 'Alas, my master! What shall we do?' So he answered, 'Do not fear, for those who are with us are more than those who are with them.' And Elisha prayed, and said, 'Lord, I pray, open his eyes that he may see.' Then the Lord opened the eyes of the young man, and he saw. And behold, the mountain was full of horses and chariots of fire all around Elisha" (II Kings 6:15-17).

Releasing the Ministry of Angelic Spirits

Intercessory prayer opens the eyes of the young servants to see the mountains full of horses and chariots. Intercessory prayer also releases the ministry of angelic ministering spirits.

Intercessory prayer recognizes the invisible world of the angelic creation and knows that they are there to serve the believer. They have been called in sacred service, and they are to be, in some ways, our heavenly pastors. Angels are inferior to saints. They have holiness, dignity and great status, yet are sent by Christ's commands to minister. (See Hebrews 13:2.)

"But to which of the angels has He ever said: 'Sit at My right hand, till I make Your enemies Your footstool?' Are they not all ministering spirits sent forth to minister for those who will inherit salvation?" (Hebrews 1:13-14).

An angel is simply a messenger, a divine celestial being with a message from God, representing God from the heavenly world. The word "angel" is used over two hundred times in the New Testament. In this Scripture, angels are called "ministering spirits."

"And He was there in the wilderness forty days, tempted by Satan, and was with the wild beasts; and the angels ministered to Him" (Mark 1:13).

In the fourteenth century, the mystics calculated how many ministering angels there were. How they came up with a number, nobody knows, but interestingly enough they calculated that 301,655,722 ministering angels were discharged to help the redeemed. Regardless of whether this count is accurate or not, we know that among the angels, some are set in charge of nations, while others are companions of the faithful. There are millions of spiritual creatures walking the earth unseen, both when we wake and when we sleep. Angels are here to minister to us, and intercessory prayer releases them to do so, as we ask them to intervene with us and for us at all times and on all occasions. Angels are called to protect and deliver the righteous.

During the graveyard shift in a subway station, one of the workers leaned against a rail looking down at the subway tracks two floors below. Suddenly the rail broke, and the man plunged down twenty feet to the tracks. Horrified, the onlookers watched helplessly as a train bore down on the unconscious form lying across the tracks, directly in the path of death. As people stared in shock, something invisible picked the man's body up and threw him parallel to the tracks just as the train flew by. Unharmed and unshaken, the man stood up and asked the onlookers what had taken place. No one had an answer. After his shift the man returned home to find his six-year old daughter waiting for him with tears pouring down her face. Running to him, she threw her arms around him and cried, "Daddy, I'm so glad to see you! In the middle of the night an angel woke me up and told me to pray for your safety. I'm so glad you're alive!"

"For He shall give His angels charge over you, to keep you in all your ways. In their hands they shall bear you up, lest you dash your foot against a stone" (Psalm 91:11-12).

"And when he came to the den, he cried out with a lamenting voice to Daniel. The king spoke, saying to Daniel, 'Daniel, servant of the living God, has your God, whom you serve continually, been able to deliver you from the lions?' Then Daniel said to the king, 'Oh king, live forever! My God sent His angel and shut the lions' mouths, so that they have not hurt me, because I was found innocent before Him; and also, oh king, I have done no wrong before you' " (Daniel 6:20-22).

Here, we have angels who bear us up, protect us, do not allow us to dash our feet, or, more specifically, keep the lions' mouths shut with their angelic hands.

"So it was that the beggar died, and was carried by the angels to Abraham's bosom. The rich man also died and was buried" (Luke 16:22).

At the hour of death, the celestial escort receives the soul the moment before it leaves the body. These angelic beings are available to those who understand that intercession releases these ministering spirits. I am not at all advocating worshipping angels or praying to angels. I believe we are to pray through the Spirit unto Christ. Christ is always the person to whom we speak our prayers. But, we can ask the Holy Spirit to release angelic ministering spirits, ministering angels, that will be of service to us to protect us, helps us, keep us, watch over us and go before us. From the throne of God and from the seat of honor, commands are given to angels to work on behalf of and for the benefit of believers. They must obey and serve. They are sent by God. (See Psalm 34:7.)

Further Study

1. Why is it necessary for intercessory prayer to strike a specific target? What is the difference between praying generally and praying specifically? (List/discuss examples of both)

2. What kind of specific targets should be prayed for during intercession?

3. What does Esther 9:12-14 and Mark 10:46-52 teach us concerning intercessory prayer?

4. Intercessory prayer is needed to release healing to society's troubled waters. Specifically, what are some of the "troubled waters" of society that can be healed through prayer?

5. Describe the role of intercessory prayer in releasing the ministry of angelic spirits. What ministries do angels perform when released by prayer?

Note

1.   Frank Peretti, <u>Piercing the Darkness</u>.

Chapter Thirteen:
Expanding Boundaries to Eliminate Spiritual Enemies

God-Ordained Boundary Lines

During the time that I was preaching the series on intercession at my church, I had a life-changing experience. I had just shared on "Expanding Boundaries to Eliminate Spiritual Enemies" when I encountered a unique situation. Mike White, City Bible Church prayer pastor, who was involved in the intercession that took place on my behalf, conveys my story, here.

The silence only lasted about twenty seconds, but that was when the battle was won.

It was a regularly scheduled lay pastor meeting. A last minute change had us convening at our new downtown outreach center, instead of at the church. Lay pastor gatherings are always upbeat, enriching and loads of fun. But this particular night took a different spin.

About thirty-five of us had made our way to the Main Street building downtown. There were the typical high-fives, hugs and "shoptalk," and then Pastor Frank called the meeting to order. He covered some upcoming events and expressed his appreciation for our help in pastoring the flock. He really meant it. Then he said, "I have something I want to share that I don't want leaving this room."

He had our attention.

We were already aware that Pastor Frank was recovering from extensive knee surgery. Things were progressing as expected, but the results of the routine, pre-surgery blood work were not expected.

The lab reported that Frank had Hepatitis C. Hepatitis C has no known cure and is the most harmful of the Hepatitis family of blood diseases. While I do not remember all of the details, I do recall that this disease is very serious, often fatal, and something I hope never to have the joy of experiencing.

He had contracted the disease over twenty-three years ago, and, according to his hematologist, it had been working on his liver ever since. Early the next morning Pastor Frank was scheduled for a liver biopsy to measure the extent of the damage. Naturally, he and his wife Sharon were a little concerned.

When he had finished sharing the details, there was a silent pause . . . about twenty seconds' worth.

We all knew we were going to pray, but how. "God, give the doctors wisdom." "Please comfort Sharon and the kids." And then there were those thoughts that passed through my mind . . . the kind I would never say out loud.

But something in the atmosphere of that gathering would not allow half-hearted prayers to be spoken. It would not allow "Plan B" scenarios to be considered. And it put a resolve in our hearts that said, "If you're going after our Pastor, you'll have to go through us first."

In that short span of silence, the Holy Spirit had swept through the room and armed each of us with a supernatural faith and courage.

Then, one by one, different lay pastors rose to share what God was laying on their hearts. Prophetic encouragement was spoken, past promises reiterated and commitments to stand in faith, come what may.

We then gathered around Frank and Sharon and began to pray. We laid hands upon them as different ones led out. No less than fifteen individuals voiced prayers while the rest of us agreed.

Some prayers literally shook the room as the thundering voice of a warrior shouted out against the disease. No less effective, however, were the compassionate appeals of the more gentle natured.

The session seemed to climax when one of the young mothers of our group received a vision in which she saw herself being fitted by the Lord in surgical scrubs. She then walked over to Pastor Frank with hands raised, cleaned and prepped for surgery, and laid them next to his liver. Admittedly, this demonstration was somewhat peculiar, yet it seemed very right at the moment.

The entire affair lasted probably ninety minutes from the time Pastor Frank shared his condition until the final prayer. As we closed, embraces were exchanged; final words of support expressed and we adjourned, sensing that we had broken through.

Within forty-eight hours, the biopsy results came back. The hematologist confirmed that there was less than 5 percent damage to Pastor Frank's liver after twenty-three years of exposure to Hepatitis C.

While relating the test results, the unbelieving doctor volunteered this observation, "Whatever those people who prayed for you did, have them keep it up. This is not what I expected the biopsy to reveal."

A few weeks later, on the advice of a physician in the church, Pastor Frank asked a second doctor to review the biopsy results. The amazed physician reported back, "Indeed, there was less than 5 percent damage to your liver. Those test results reveal no damage whatsoever."

Intercessory prayer establishes true boundaries. In the Old Testament, God gave boundaries to nations, families and cities. Those boundaries were intended to stretch all the way to their furthermost reach, and the boundaries were not allowed to fall short of that mark. God still establishes boundaries today—for individuals, families, nations, churches and cities. Through intercession, we can press the borderlines out to their God-set dimensions and claim our God-given heritage.

"To the image of His Son, that He might be the firstborn among many brethren. Moreover whom He predestined, these He also called; whom He called, these He also justified; and whom He justified, these He also glorified" (Romans 8:29-30).

The word "predestined," here, means "before boundaries were set." The boundaries for each of our lives were set by God's divine wisdom. God has a predetermined, unique destiny for each life. God has given each one of us a great spiritual capacity to grow and stretch and believe. For each person He foreknew, He predestined and assigned boundary lines. God knows our exact make-up, both physically and spiritually. He knows what goals we should accomplish in life, what visions we should fulfill. These spiritual boundary lines apply not only to each individual life, but to each church, city and nation as well.

"You have hedged me behind and before, and laid Your hand upon me. Such knowledge is too wonderful for me; it is high, I cannot attain it" (Psalm 139:5-6).

Pushing Back the Devil's Boundary Lines

The Holy Spirit has hedged us in according to God's divinely set boundary lines. The devil also sets boundary lines, but his boundary lines are always to shrink us, to bind us, to pull us back and to remove from us the spirit of faith and vision. These boundary lines that the devil clamps on our lives come through bad experiences. The devil can even set boundary lines upon our lives based on generational sins and generational experiences.

Through faith and intercessory prayer, we are to move the boundary lines back to God's prescribed position. If you fear that your life is a waste or is painfully limited, if you are dissatisfied and there seems to be nothing you can do about it, if you feel trapped, with no options, and think that life is all over for you, then you have been squeezed, limited.

> # God has given us a 5,000 acre farm to live on and the devil tries to shrink us to one acre.

Your boundary lines have been moved back by demonic forces. This work of the devil strives to ruin your life, cause you to accept the narrow box he has put you in. Through intercessory prayer, you need to believe Jeremiah 29:11.

"For I know the thoughts that I think toward you, says the Lord, thoughts of peace and not of evil, to give you a future and a hope" (Jeremiah 29:11). (See Psalms 37:23, 31:8; Proverbs 18:16.)

Extending Your Boundaries

The Holy Spirit, through intercessory prayer, will give you a capacity to extend your borderlines. God has given us a 5,000-acre farm on which to live, and the devil tries to shrink us to one acre. Through intercessory prayer, we begin to sense the true borderlines, faith grows and our intercession has a goal and vision to it that was not there before. The true borderlines are restored not only for our own lives, but also for our families, our friends, our churches, our cities and, ultimately, our nations.

Billy Sunday used to ask his congregation, "How many of you have personally met the devil today? If you have not met the devil today face to face, then you are probably going the same direction that he is." We are to push back the devil's boundaries, go against him and extend our borders into his territory.

"Not that I have already attained, or am already perfected; but I press on, that I may lay hold of that for which Christ Jesus has also laid hold of me" (Philippians 3:12).

The Apostle Paul had a mark to reach, a boundary line to stretch into. We must give up our small ambitions, reject mediocrity and stretch beyond the limitations that our minds have accepted. The word "push" in Philippians 3:12 means "to press violently, to push one's way into, to pursue, to speed on as in a race." We are to stretch or push out strenuously, powerfully to reach God's expectations for us by any means necessary.

The Hebrew word for "border" means "a cord twisted and set around an object to show a set boundary, a territory enclosed by fences, landmarks and walls, something that has received its limitations." There is a difference between God's border for our lives, our own borders and the devil's snares and his borders.

Spiritual borders are often different from natural borders. The spiritual influence of a church or city may reach far beyond its designated borders. We must learn to discern spiritual borders by the boundaries of influence.

The enemy silently and slowly limits our vision and, like a snake coiled around us, tries to crush us. Satan places boundaries around our lives so slowly and subtly that we do not notice it is happening. When a python catches a bird, he does not immediately swallow it. He curls up around it and begins a slow process of crushing it. After the snake coils his body around the terrified bird, he pauses, waits. Panicked, the little bird draws in a big breath, then breathes out. As the bird's ribcage contracts, the snake's hold tightens with the movement. The bird gasps again, then exhales, and the snake again tightens his hold. Each time the bird breathes in, the serpent waits. When the bird breathes out, the snake coils tighter. Each breath is a little shallower; each exhalation brings the coil in a little tighter. Finally the bird can no longer gasp for air and soon dies.

Satan does the same thing to our lives. He coils his boundaries around our lives; then he begins to squeeze . . . for weeks, months, years. We take in a big breath, and think we are going to be all right. Then we breathe out, and he closes in a little more. Each time he closes in more tightly, until we are used to being coiled around, closed in, snared. Gradually we begin to think that it is normal to be unable to breathe. Constricted boundaries feel natural. Bondage seems normal.

But intercessory prayer pushes the lines back to where God has ordained them to be. Intercessors sense the work of the enemy, but they also realize God's destiny for the situation. God has always set generous boundary lines for each individual, for His people, but that inheritance was only reached through prayer warfare. In Joshua 19, the Hebrew word for intercession, as we have already defined in chapter two, is the word *paga*. This same Hebrew word is translated in Joshua 19 as "reached." The terms "intercession" and "reached" give a clear picture of outermost borderlines reached through intercessory prayer. (See Joshua 19:22, 26-27, 34.)

"Their border went toward the west and to Maralah, went to Dabbasheth, and extended along the brook that is east of Jokneam" (Joshua 19:11).

Establishing Our "God-Ordained" Boundaries

As God has given each one of us an inheritance, we need to reach our furthestmost borderlines through spiritual warfare. As we engage in intercessory prayer, God urges us to stretch out, to break out.

We are to remove satanic limitations.

These limit our personal, family and business lives. They stop spiritual growth. Satanic limitations cause grief, sorrow, worry, doubt, and fear. These are not of God's making. They are caused by negative strongholds, and they must be removed. (See Judges 15:13, 16:6-8; Leviticus 14:7; Isaiah 52:2, 58:6; John 11:44; Ecclesiastics 12:6.)

We are to spiritually stretch and enlarge.

Self-imposed boundaries must also be broken–carnality, sin, negative personality traits, double-mindedness and anything that lessens what we obtain of the supernatural vision God wants us to have. (See Genesis 9:27; Deuteronomy 12:20, 19:8; I Chronicles 4:10; Psalm 119:32; Isaiah 54:1-2.)

We are to remove all spiritual parasites.

A parasite lives off a host, giving nothing in return. A parasite attaches itself to a healthy system to drain off energy and life. A parasite clings to another and extracts whatever it can for its own advantage.

- We need to remove the parasite of insecurity: those circumstances or experiences that cause us to doubt God or His Word, ourselves, our worth or the hope of a fulfilled life.
- We need to remove the parasite of fear: those experiences that cause hurt and doubt, such as unanswered prayer or death instead of healing. These are areas that open us up to the spirit of fear.
- We need to remove the parasite of emotional coldness: those generational or personality strongholds which cripple the ability to respond emotionally or to show emotion.
- We need to remove the parasite of spiritual exhaustion: the physical and emotional exhaustion from over-scheduled lives. Physical exhaustion affects our spiritual being, destroys our will to press to the borderlines that God has given us.

ESTABLISHING OUR "GOD-ORDAINED" BOUNDARIES

- **We are to remove Satanic limitations.**
  Judges 15:13, 16:6-8;Leviticus 14:7; Isaiah 52:2, 58:6; John 11:44; Ecclesiastics 12:6.

- **We are to spiritually stretch and enlarge.**
  Genesis 9:27; Deuteronomy 12:20, 19:8; I Chronicles 4: 10; Psalm 119:32, Isaiah 54: 1-2.

- **We are to remove all spiritual parasites.**

Elimination of Spiritual Enemies

The word *paga* in the Hebrew means "to attack, to fall upon or to encounter the enemy." This aspect of *paga*-praying is the readiness of God's servant to do his Master's will, to attack his Master's enemies upon command.

It is a prayer assault on darkness, principalities and powers, a call to spiritual-warfare-praying. In Judges 8:21, the word *paga* is used in this warfare context.

"So Zebah and Zalmunna said, 'Rise yourself, and kill us; for as a man is, so is his strength.' So Gideon arose and killed Zebah and Zalmunna, and took the crescent ornaments that were on their camels' necks" (Judges 8:21).

This spirit of intercessory prayer, seen here in the natural realm, applies in the spiritual realm. The spirit of intercessory prayer rises up against spiritual enemies, falls upon them, attacking them to destroy them.

"Then the king said to the guards who stood about him, 'Turn and kill the priests of the Lord, because their hand also is with David, and because they knew when he fled and did not tell it to me.' But the servants of the king would not lift their hands to strike the priests of the Lord. And the king said to Doeg, 'You turn and kill the priests!' So Doeg the Edomite turned and struck the priests, and killed on that day eighty-five men who wore a linen ephod" (I Samuel 22:17-18).

This is a sad story in Scripture. But, again, the word *paga* is illustrated as the ability to turn immediately and to kill (*paga*) the enemy. We are to have this same spirit. What Doeg did unrighteously, we are to do righteously.

The Attack Attitude

Picture yourself in the following situation. As you pull into your driveway and get out of your car, you see movement inside your home. Your family is with you in the car, so you know thieves are breaking into your house! You run to the neighbor's house to call the police. Anxiously you wait, hoping they arrive before the thieves leave with your valuables. Down the street you hear the sirens. Police cars screech to a halt in front of your house. Officers jump out of their cars and run to the curb, where they line up and begin to sing. *Sing?*

You listen closely. They are singing about how they have the authority to stop the robbers and how they can regain your possessions. Meanwhile, the thieves rob you blind.[1]

This is often a picture of the Church today. We sing about attacking the enemy, we talk about it, preach about it, but we do not actually do it.

We must put action behind our words and intentions—we must attack the enemy!

The Ichneumon Attack Attitude

The ichneumon is a small animal that can overcome and destroy king cobra snakes that are more than three feet long. But the ichneumon only attacks a snake when it is near a certain plant whose leaves contain an antidote for snakebite. When bitten, the little creature immediately retreats to the lifesaving plant and nibbles on its leaves. Once restored, it is ready to renew the attack. Each time it is bitten, it goes to the plant, and then returns to fight the enemy.

In the same way, the only way we can be successful in our attack during intercession is to know that our power is in Christ. As we fight the enemy and get wounded, we must continually return to Christ for strength and renewing. Then we can again return to fight the enemy.

Spiritual Enemies to Attack

We must attack numerous spiritual enemies. We must attack offensively, not defensively. Let us run to the battle, as David ran toward Goliath!

Attack Passivity

"Oh well, things are the way they are, and there is nothing I can do about it." The readiness to attack the enemy requires faith, confidence and action.

Attack Procrastination

"Maybe the enemy will go away. I'll do it in a while. The situation is not bad enough yet to take action. " A true attacking, *paga*, intercessory prayer does not put off until tomorrow what needs to be done today.

Attack Panicked Confusion

We must, with faith and direction, attack those enemies that bring harm to our spirits and to those around us. We must be willing to penetrate, change, make headway into the enemy's camp, into his strongholds. It is a Gideon spirit with a barley loaf rolling down the hill to scatter the enemy.

Attack Timidity

We know who we are and where we stand. We must learn how to fight and conquer. We cannot live in fear or intimidation. We must not live on the defensive, but on the offensive. We are moving in to attack the gates of hell. We are not stationary, living in a fortress, waiting for the enemy to attack us. We are on the offensive, looking for ways to penetrate the kingdom of darkness and attack the enemy.

That willingness to attack the enemy comes from our position in Christ, from the victory won at the cross by the Lord Jesus, from His righteousness and His ability to attack through us. The willingness to attack in intercession requires pushing the enemy back persistently, and not giving up because the enemy retaliates in some way–when the enemy finds that we do not have on all of our armor and we are attacked in a weak place. The *paga* attitude of intercessory prayer presses against the enemy at all times, with all faith, to bring about a victory that only intercessory prayer can bring about.

These five basic goals of intercessory prayer–interceding with spiritual travail, striking the target, obtaining supernatural assistance, setting divine boundary lines, and eliminating the enemy–which were reviewed in the past three chapters, are goals that every believer can use and that every church should use. We can perfect these to highly fine-tuned weapons and put them in our arsenal of intercessory prayer ministry so that we can launch against the kingdom of darkness.

Further Study

1. What does it mean to be limited by satanic boundary lines? Specifically, how can Satan limit an individual or church?

2. Describe/discuss the role of prayer in pushing back the boundary lines of Satan. What boundary lines would you like to push back in your own life?

3. What does it mean to have God-ordained boundaries?

4. What does it mean to have an attack attitude in prayer? What are some of the attitudes (i.e.. spiritual enemies) that we should attack in prayer?

Note

1.   Dean Sherman.

Chapter Fourteen:
Empowered by the Holy Spirit

A sense of urgency flooded Vickie's spirit. At ten o'clock on that Saturday morning, while cleaning house, she was suddenly intensely concerned about her teenage son who was camping with friends that weekend. She immediately dropped to her knees and began to pray as the Holy Spirit prompted her. After an hour of intense praying, she rose from her knees and resumed her housework.

The next day her son came home, shaken by an accident that had taken place the day before. He had been standing by a swift river when his foot slipped and he fell down a steep embankment into the strong current. The water swept him down river toward a fifty-foot waterfall. He frantically reached out to boulders he hurtled past. Suddenly the current trapped him against a large boulder. He clutched at the moss-covered rock, desperately trying to find a crack to wedge his fingers into. The next instant he found himself standing on top of the boulder, with no knowledge of how he had gotten there. The time? Ten o'clock Saturday morning.

The Holy Spirit had alerted his interceding mother and had turned sure tragedy into triumph. Intercession is most successful when it is directed by the Holy Spirit. All kingdom activities are in the Holy Spirit's realm.

"For the kingdom of God is not eating and drinking, but righteousness and peace and joy in the Holy Spirit" (Romans 14:17).

If we were to excise the middle part of the verse, Romans 14:17 would read, "For the Kingdom of God is . . . in the Holy Spirit." The life of the Kingdom is in the power and life of the Holy Spirit, so intercessory prayer finds its life and power in the Holy Sprit. To pray without the unction of the Holy Spirit results in a lifeless, formalistic prayer. When a person, church or group of people loses the life and anointing of the Holy Spirit, prayer will become a dead form of Church tradition. It is no surprise that prayer meetings in the past have suffered from poor attendance. Prayer must be carried along on the wings of the Spirit. When living prayers are offered by spiritually alive people, there is a spiritual combustion, powerful praying.

Archbishop Trench (1807-1886), the great biblical expositor and Greek scholar, said, "We must pray in the Spirit if we would pray at all. Lay this, I beseech, to heart. Do not address yourselves to prayer as a work to be accomplished in your own natural strength. It is the work of God, the Holy Ghost, a work in you and by you and in which you must be fellows workers with Him."

Spirit-Empowered Intercession in the Early Church

In the New Testament, the Church prayed spontaneous prayers by, in, and through the Holy Spirit. The beginning of a Christian life is marked by the indwelling Spirit crying out to God, "*Abba.*" (See Galatians 4:6; Romans 8:15.) On all occasions, the Scriptures encourage the believer, pray "in the Spirit" and "by the Spirit." This injunction applies to every kind of praying, especially intercessory prayer. (See Ephesians 6:18.)

"Likewise the Spirit also helps in our weaknesses. For we do not know what we should pray for as we ought, but the Spirit Himself makes intercession for us with groanings which cannot be uttered. Now He who searches the hearts knows what the mind of the Spirit is, because He makes intercession for the saints according to the will of God" (Romans 8:26-27).

The Holy Spirit is a person, so personal pronouns like "He" and "Him" are biblical norms. The Spirit's lordship is, in effect, the lordship of Christ, who sent the Spirit to be our other helper. The Holy Spirit is not merely a divine influence or power, but a person. The Holy Spirit is mentioned some 90 times, with 18 different titles in the Old Testament, and 260 times with 39 titles in the New Testament.

The Holy Spirit is referred to as "He." This is the same appellation used of Jehovah in the Old Testament.

"Sow for yourselves righteousness; reap in mercy; break up your fallow ground, for it is time to seek the Lord, till He comes and rains righteousness on you" (Hosea 10:12).

The New Testament uses this title also to refer to Christ. "I indeed baptize you with water unto repentance, but He who is coming after me is mightier than I, whose sandals I am not worthy to carry. He will baptize you with the Holy Spirit and fire" (Matthew 3:11).

This title "He" is used eighteen times in referring to the Holy Spirit: "And I will pray the Father, and He will give you another Helper, that He may abide with you forever" (John 14:16).

"However, when He, the Spirit of truth, has come, He will guide you into all truth; for He will not speak on His own authority, but whatever He hears He will speak; and He will tell you things to come. He will glorify Me, for He will take of what is Mine and declare it to you. All things that the Father has are Mine. Therefore I said that He will take of Mine and declare it to you" (John 16:13-15).

Spirit-Empowered Intercession for Every Believer

The Holy Spirit comes to indwell every believer.

We are not left alone as orphans, visited only rarely by the Holy Spirit. He now abides in us as our partner, companion, helper. Conversion from unbelief to belief begins with hearing the gospel, appropriating it by faith and then experiencing the receiving of the Holy Spirit. (See I Corinthians 3:16, 19.) (See also Galatians 3:2-5, 5:5; II Corinthians 4:13.)

"Not by works of righteousness which we have done, but according to His mercy He saved us, through the washing of regeneration and renewing of the Holy Spirit" (Titus 3:5).

The Holy Spirit teaches us how to pray.

In prayer, the Holy Spirit is our mentor, our guide, our equipper. In our present state of weakness, we do not know how or what to pray, but the Spirit knows.

"Likewise the Spirit also helps in our weaknesses. For we do not know what we should pray for as we ought, but the Spirit Himself makes intercession for us with groanings which cannot be uttered. Now He who searches the heart knows what the mind of the Spirit is, because He makes intercession for the saints according to the will of God" (Romans 8:26-27).

The Holy Spirit has complete freedom of movement.

The Spirit cannot be located, weighed or dissected; He is immaterial. Since the Spirit knows no corporeal limitations, He can be everywhere at once. He is without limitations. Our human experiences are limited by our physical bodies, but the Holy Spirit is not. The Holy Spirit is not bound by places or things, but is free to move anywhere instantly. For intercessory prayer, this is awesome!

"Now the Lord is the Spirit; and where the Spirit of the Lord is, there is liberty" (II Corinthians 3:17).

The Holy Spirit possesses energy, drive and dynamic movement. (See Luke 1:35.) This same energy, drive and dynamic movement rests upon the intercessor in prayer. The Holy Spirit will, at times, overshadow the believer and energize him or her for dynamic movement in the spirit realm. Because He is without limitation, so also, we in prayer may travel by the Spirit to any nation.

"But if I cast out demons by the Spirit of God, surely the kingdom of God has come upon you" (Matthew 12:28).

The Holy Spirit is a vital force, with a power far beyond any imaginable human power.

"Wind" and "breath" depict the Spirit of God as a moving force, a divine kind of energy. At the inception of creation, a force moved over the primeval waters. That force was the Holy Spirit. When the Holy Spirit moves by force, the creation of God takes place. Intercessory prayer has this force behind, in, and around its praying. Holy Spirit-inspired prayer has the force of God, the same force as seen in Genesis 1:2: "The earth was without form, and void; and darkness was on the face of the deep. And the Spirit of God was hovering over the face of the waters." (See also Acts 2:2.)

The unaided man cannot accomplish true intercession.

The Holy Spirit is our empowering force as we go to prayer. The Holy Spirit breathes into us a desire for prayer, gives us power in prayer, enables us to persevere in prayer. The unaided man cannot accomplish true intercession. Intercession is "by the Spirit," "in the Spirit," and "through the Spirit." (See I Corinthians 2:14.)

"Praying always with all prayer and supplication in the Spirit, being watchful to this end with all perseverance and supplication for all the saints" (Ephesians 6:18).

The Greek phrase "in the Spirit" means we are to be totally immersed, completely surrounded by the Spirit. This is the description of a biblical intercessory prayer meeting. The Spirit is the atmosphere of our intercession, the transforming power-force around and in us. We breathe the atmosphere of the Holy Spirit and, thus, pray Holy Spirit thoughts, words, emotions, insights, burdens and moods. The Holy Spirit bestows a spirit of grace upon our intercession that causes a divine enablement, a supernatural release of God's ability in us. When we cannot accomplish difficult intercession, the Spirit of grace empowers and pushes us in the Holy Spirit's strength and force.

"So he answered and said to me: 'This is the word of the Lord to Zerubbabel: "Not by might nor by power, but by My Spirit," says the Lord of hosts. "Who are you, oh great mountain? Before Zerubbabel you shall become a plain! And he shall bring forth the capstone with shouts of 'Grace, grace to it!' " ' " (Zechariah 4:6-7).

Intercessory prayer is empowered by the grace of God.

Grace is the compassionate response of one who is able to help another person in need. In the natural realm it speaks of helping someone who is incapable of helping himself. The Holy Spirit becomes our spirit of might and strength. Our natural might is limited. True spiritual intercession moves from natural might into spiritual might.

The Hebrew word used in Zechariah 4:6, "not by might," means "stretched to the limits, to the breaking point." We need supernatural enablement during each intercessory prayer time. The Holy Spirit Himself must be present all through our praying to help our weaknesses of flesh and mind and to give life and power.

"That He would grant you, according to the riches of His glory, to be strengthened with might through His Spirit in the inner man" (Ephesians 3:16).

Intercessory prayer has the empowering presence of an advocate.

The Holy Spirit is our advocate, aide, personal mentor, helping us make proper intercession. The Holy Spirit is described as our "Comforter"–the Greek reads, *paraklete*, "one who is called to our side to aid, help, counsel, guide and defend"–and this suggests the capability and adaptability to bring aid anywhere at anytime. The *paraklete* helped the defendant understand the issues before him, helped him clearly see the issues at stake, and then suggested the course of action to take. This is how intercessory prayer succeeds. We have our own personal mentor who knows what to say, how to say it, and what are the real issues at hand. Intercession takes us to a new level, when the Holy Spirit empowers our time before the throne of God. (See John 15:26.)

"But the Helper, the Holy Spirit, whom the Father will send in My name, He will teach you all things, and bring to your remembrance all things that I said to you" (John 14:26).

Intercessory Prayer and the Believer's Spiritual Language

Intercessory prayer, aided and directed by the Holy Spirit, is further strengthened by using one's spiritual language. I realize that this is not embraced by all, for many various reasons. I hesitated to include this section in this book, not desiring to separate any of my Christian brothers or sisters who pray fervently and successfully without speaking in a spiritual language. However, I do personally see this as a profound and wonderful aid to intercessory prayer. Gordon Fee in his book, *Paul, the Spirit and the People of God*, connects intercessory prayer and speaking in tongues:

> With prayer in particular, the Spirit helps us in our already/not yet existence. Because in our present weakness we do not know how or for what to pray, the Spirit Himself makes intercession for us with inarticulate groanings (Romans 8:26-27), an expression that most likely refers to *glossolalia*, speaking in tongues. Prayer and praise, therefore, seems the best way to view Paul's understanding of *glossolalia*. At no point in I Corinthians 14 does Paul suggest that tongues is speech directed toward people; three times he indicates that it is speech directed toward God (I Corinthians 14:2, 14-16, 28). In I Corinthians 14:14-16 he specifically refers to tongues as "praying with my spirit," and in I Corinthians 14:2 such prayer is described as "speaking mysteries to God," which is why the mind of the speaker is left unfruitful, and also why such prayer without interpretation is not to be part of the corporate setting. Paul himself engaged in such prayer so frequently that he can boldly say to a congregation who treasured the gift that he prayed in tongues more than any of them (I Corinthians 14:18). To be sure, he will also, he insists, "pray with my mind." What he

will not do is engage in only one form of prayer, as most later Christians have tended to do.[1]

Filled With the Spirit and The Believer's Spiritual Language

Speaking one's spiritual language and being filled with the Holy Spirit seem to work together. Phrases that denote being "baptized in the Spirit" and "filled with the Spirit" are used interchangeably as related to aspects of the same experience. Baptism with the Holy Spirit results in one being filled to overflowing with the presence and power of the Holy Spirit.

"To be filled with the Spirit is an expansion of our capacity for worshipping, an extension of our dynamic for witnessing and an expulsion of the adversary through our spiritual warfare" (Jack Hayford).[2]

The believer receives the presence and power of the Holy Spirit within himself until the Holy Spirit wells up within him and flows forth like a river from within the innermost depths of his person. (See Luke 11:11-13.)

"On the last day, that great day of the feast, Jesus stood and cried out, saying, 'If anyone thirsts, let him come to Me and drink. He who believes in Me, as the Scripture has said, out of his heart will flow rivers of living water'" (John 7:37-38).

Receiving a Spiritual Language

Receiving a spiritual language from the Holy Spirit enhances the believer's own personal relationship to the Lord Jesus. The Holy Spirit speaks through the believer in languages never learned before by the speaker. The New Testament refers to this spiritual language as "other tongues," "new tongues," and "diverse kinds of tongues." The phrases "filled with the Spirit" and "praying in the Spirit" are the same in the biblical Greek: *en pneumati*, meaning "in the spiritual realm and with the Holy Spirit's aid." (See I Corinthians 14:4,14.)

"For he who speaks in a tongue does not speak to men but to God, for no one understands him; however, in the spirit he speaks mysteries" (I Corinthians 14:2).

The gift of tongues, which differs from praying in the Spirit, and is referred to in I Corinthians 12:11, is given by the sovereign will of the Holy Spirit. It cannot be gained by human initiative or intervention and is not given to every believer. (See I Corinthians 12:30.) It is used with the gift of interpretation. (See I Corinthians 12:10, 12:28, 30, 13:8.)

The Holy Spirit Prays Through Our Spiritual Languages

The believer's spiritual language allows the Holy Spirit to pray through us when we do not know how to pray or what to pray. During intercessory prayer times, the Spirit may choose to utilize the believer's spiritual language when there are definite prayer targets. The mind may know the direction of the prayer, but the Spirit, using spiritual language, may make requests, and have insights not known in the natural realm by the pray-er.

"Likewise the Spirit also helps in our weaknesses. For we do not know what we should pray for as we ought, but the Spirit Himself makes intercession for us with groanings which cannot be uttered. Now He who searches the heart knows what the mind of the Spirit is, because He makes intercession for the saints according to the will of God. And we know that all things work together for good to those who love God, to those who are the called according to His purpose" (Romans 8:26-28).

- We may use our spiritual languages to pray for the spiritual warfare of others.
- We may use our spiritual languages to pray for the physical protection and well-being of someone in known danger, or to pray when we do not know anything but the burden of the Spirit leading us into a season of intercession.
- We may use our spiritual languages to intercede for the ministries of others and, especially, for missionaries when communication may be difficult or impossible.

The Apostle Paul testified that he spoke in tongues more than the tongue-speaking Corinthian church. (See I Corinthians 14:18.) Spiritual language obviously played a significant role in Paul's private devotions, his intercession for churches, his ministry team and the continual warfare of the soul. Paul speaks with reverence and gratitude of this manifestation of the Holy Spirit. If we are to use the prayer language biblically, certainly we should let the words of Paul, Spirit-inspired apostle and teacher, inform our doctrine and practice. In I Corinthians 14:2 Paul teaches that the Holy Spirit aids in the prayer of intercession with His personal insights.

"For he who speaks in a tongue does not speak to men but to God, for no one understands him; however, in the spirit he speaks mysteries" (I Corinthians 14:2).

Directing Our Spiritual Languages

Prayer-intercession, using our spiritual languages, is directed toward God, in the Spirit and of the Spirit. It is spirit to Spirit without the interruption of the human mind and without the limitation of the human reasoning, with its doubts and limited vision. Spiritual language speaks in mysteries far greater than natural comprehension, mysteries that can be spoken only by divine revelation. Intercession with our spiritual language allows the Holy Spirit to reveal His insights to our minds.

Our prayer-intercession with the spiritual language has a personal spiritual benefit. "He who speaks in a tongue edifies himself, but he who prophesies edifies the church." (I Corinthians 14:4).

To edify is to build up something, stabilize, strengthen. When we engage in fervent prayer with speaking in tongues, our spirits are edified, our minds are renewed and our strength is replenished. "But you, beloved, building yourselves up on your most holy faith, praying in the Holy Spirit . . ." (Jude 1:20).

Praying in the Spirit and by the Spirit mysteriously rebuilds something in the pray-er. The Holy Spirit restores and rebuilds in us what life, crisis or warfare have torn down. The Holy Spirit renews our perspectives, revives our vision and instructs our minds. Truth is more easily assimilated by our spirits as we intercede with spiritual languages.

"To whom He said, 'This is the rest with which you may cause the weary to rest,' and, 'This is the refreshing'; yet they would not hear" (Isaiah 28:12).

Partnering With the Holy Spirit Using Our Spiritual Languages

Our prayer-intercession using our spiritual languages is a partnership with the Holy Spirit. The Holy Spirit is the best teacher of intercessory prayer. As we continually yield to His leading, we will grow in the school of intercession.

> Our prayer intercession using our spiritual language is a partnership with the Holy Spirit.

"For if I pray in a tongue, my spirit prays, but my understanding is unfruitful" (I Corinthians 14:14).

Man speaks through his understanding, but not with a spiritual language. The expression "my understanding is unfruitful," means that the mind does not intellectually share in the blessing that is occurring in man's spirit. The insight of this verse is that the Spirit prays through us about things we do not, in our natural state, understand, and for which we do not know how to pray. This is when the prayer language becomes a powerful tool of prayer-intercession: praying in our spiritual language on a supernatural level, beyond the limitations of the human mind or human reasoning. For we do not know how to pray as we should, but the Spirit Himself intercedes for us with groanings too deep for words. The Holy Spirit bypasses us and improves the accuracy of our praying. Intercession is learning to pray on target. The Holy Spirit is the coach; we are the archers, with our arrows notched and ready to shoot. The Holy Spirit guides our arrows to the target as we intercede with our spiritual languages.

During our prayer-intercession, we may desire to use our spiritual language in praise and worship. We may mix "singing in the Spirit" with "speaking in the Spirit."

"What is the conclusion then? I will pray with the spirit, and I will also pray with the understanding. I will sing with the spirit, and I will also sing with the understanding" (I Corinthians 14:15).

A supernatural, spiritual strengthening occurs as we sing in tongues. The Apostle Paul encourages giving thanks to God through our spiritual language. No doubt he employed this often in his prayer-intercession. Praising and magnifying God through a spiritual language creates an atmosphere in which prayer-intercession will flow with great ease, quickened by the Holy Spirit.

"For they heard them speak with tongues and magnify God" (Acts 10:46).

We need spiritually alive prayers; prayers empowered by the Holy Spirit, to become powerful prayer-intercessors! *Oh God, that you would send your Holy Spirit to teach and empower us to pray. Let us see your power and presence, as we intercede on behalf of our churches, cities, nations, and world.*

Further Study

1. What can we learn about Spirit-empowered intercession in the early church?

2. What role should the Holy Spirit play in intercession for every believer? How does the Holy Spirit direct our prayers?

3. What does it mean to pray in a spiritual language? What role does this form of prayer have in intercessory prayer?

Notes

1.   Gordon Fee, <u>Paul, The Spirit and The People of God</u>.

2.   Jack Hayford, <u>Spiritfilled</u> (Carol Stream, IL: Tyndale Publishers, 1971), 8.

Chapter Fifteen:
Empowered by the Fasting

Prayer-intercession is empowered not only by the Holy Spirit, but also by true biblical fasting. With revival sweeping the nations, we are hearing of more prayer with fasting than prayer without fasting. We must return to the early church discipline of fasting. This discipline will be part of our training for the Church, especially in the coming generations.

Fasting has been viewed as a thing of the past, something that the early church monks did, but not something for today. Today, however, we see a renewed emphasis on fasting and prayer. For example, Bill Bright is calling two million Americans to fast for their nation.

The trumpet call to fasting is being heard throughout the world. This is the decade of fasting and prayer.

"Blow the trumpet in Zion, consecrate a fast, call a sacred assembly" (Joel 2:15).

This is the trumpet call from the Spirit, a communication from the Kingdom of Heaven. In Numbers 10:1-16, Israel was given the law, establishing times and occasions to sound the trumpet.

- Trumpet to signal the congregation to gather. (See Numbers 10:3.)
- Trumpet to signal leaders to gather. (See Numbers 10:4.)
- Trumpet to signal advancement of the camp. (See Numbers 10:5.)
- Trumpet to signal alarm, or preparation for war. (See Numbers 10:8-9.)
- Trumpet to sound over the New Year and offerings. (See Numbers 10:1.)

Today, the trumpet call of the Spirit is clear. We are to prepare for the future with a great deal of prayer and fasting. Congregations and leaders are responding worldwide. The prayer of intercession with fasting will prepare the Church for the next millennium.

...prayer of intercession with fasting will prepare the Church for the next millennium.

Intercessory prayer, joined with fasting, increases the spiritual alertness and effectiveness of God's people.

Fasting is defined as "voluntary abstinence from food for the purpose of dedicated and concentrated prayer."

Fasting in Judaism
- There was one official fast given by Yahweh (Day of Atonement).
- After the Babylonian captivity, the pious Jews established a twice-weekly fast (Monday and Thursday) which soon turned into a dead ritual.
- The Gentiles recognized fasting as a mark of a Jew.
- After the destruction of the Temple in 70 AD, fasting, more or less, replaced sacrifice for the Jew.

Church history records that certain days of fasting were established shortly after the first century. Many church fathers emphasized fasting and practiced it in their own lives, but it eventually became a dead ritual, a form without the power, as it did in Judaism.

Fasting in Church History
- Wednesdays and Fridays became regular fast days, as did the Easter fast and the fast of Lent.
- Baptismal candidates and those baptizing were also required to fast before the baptismal service.
- Polycarp (110 AD) said that fasting was a powerful aid against temptation and fleshly lusts.
- Tertullian (210 AD) said that fasting was an aid in controlling passions.
- Martin Luther not only maintained the spiritual discipline of fasting one day each week, but additionally fasted so often–along with his three hours of daily prayer–that he was often criticized for fasting too much.
- Calvin said that fasting should be used as a restraint on the flesh, as a preparation for prayer or as a testimony of our humiliation before God.

- John Knox, who had a great impact on Britain and moved the world toward God, wrestled day and night in prayer and fasted regularly.
- Wesley required all ministers to promise to fast. He required all Methodists to fast Wednesday and Fridays until about four o'clock in the afternoon.
- Charles G. Finney fasted every week. Probably the greatest and most anointed soul-winner since the Apostle Paul, Finney would spend another two or three days in fasting and prayer whenever he sensed the work of God slowing down or less of the power of God on his ministry. He testified that with fasting, the power was always restored.
- The Azusa Street Revival (1906), came as a result of a ten-day period of prayer and fasting. All revivals have followed extensive periods of fasting and prayer.

Vital Truths for Fasting

Ancient people recognized that abstaining from food brought them closer to the spiritual realm than any other process. Fasting was practiced extensively by the mystic cults and religions of antiquity, as well as by the Jews and members of the early church.

The seven deadly sins recognized throughout church history are pride, covetousness, envy, sloth, lust, gluttony and anger. Gregory the Great (540-604 AD) described these as "a classification of the normal perils of the soul in the ordinary conditions of life." Each sin is an example of a legitimate desire gone wrong. Our legitimate desire for food has degenerated into a craving for food, a bondage to food and some out-of-control behavior. The discipline of fasting teaches us much about ourselves, our drives, our character and our ability to control our bodies, our minds and our emotions. Fasting may reveal an inability to restore the importance food to its rightful place, under the control of our spirits. Fasting reaffirms our utter dependence upon God, finding Him a source of sustenance beyond food. People who combine intercessory prayer with fasting will find a new level of God's wisdom, presence and power.

"Being full of the Holy Spirit does not necessarily cause one to walk in the power of the Spirit. I believe the way into power... is to fast and pray" (Paul Yonggi Cho).[1]

"The early church called a fast statio, because he who fasted had to wait in prayer day and night like a soldier at his post" (Keil and Delitzch).[2]

"Faith needs a life of prayer in which to pray and keep strong. Prayer needs fasting for its full and perfect development. It is only in a life of moderation and temperance and self-denial that there will be the heart or the strength to pray much. We are creatures of the senses: fasting helps to express, to depend and to confirm the resolution that we are ready to sacrifice anything, to sacrifice ourselves, to attain what we seek for the Kingdom of God" (Andrew Murray).[3]

"If fasting was practiced in the churches today to the extent it is practiced in the Orient and among heathen, there is every indication that the Church of Jesus Christ would be blessed with major signs, healings and miracles all of the time instead of just a sprinkling here and there" (Franklin Hall).[4]

"Our ability to perceive God's direction is directly related to our ability to sense the inner promptings of His Holy Spirit. God provides a specific activity to assist us in doing this–fasting" (Bill Gothard).[5]

Wrong Fasting

In studying fasting and intercessory prayer, one must read Isaiah 58. Verses 1-5 expose the characteristics of the wrong kind of fast.

"Cry aloud, spare not; lift up your voice like a trumpet; tell My people their transgression, and the house of Jacob their sins. Yet they seek Me daily, and delight to know My ways, as a nation that did righteousness, and did not forsake the ordinance of their God. They ask of Me the ordinances of justice; they take delight in approaching God. 'Why have we fasted,' they say, 'and You have not seen? Why have we afflicted our souls, and You take no notice?' In fact, in the day of your fast you find pleasure, and exploit all your laborers. Indeed you fast for strife and debate, and to strike with the fist of wickedness. You will not fast as you do this day, to make your voice heard on high. Is it a fast that I have chosen, a day for a man to afflict his soul? Is it to bow down his head like a bulrush, and to spread out sackcloth and ashes? Would you call this a fast, and an acceptable day to the Lord?" (Isaiah 58:1-5).

Isaiah 58 warns against misguided fasting, when the true purpose of fasting is lost and it becomes a religious duty, causing pride and self-importance. Isaiah 58 reveals some flaws concerning Israel's rituals of fasting that certainly could apply to Christians worldwide. Since the people of Israel had, as their object, the achievement of a measure of merit, their fasting was not spiritually motivated but only performed out of duty, and this produced an irritable, edgy community. The people had fasted, but God took no interest in their religious exercises. While they were fasting, they hired servants and laborers to work long hours to make up for the fast. They put heavy burdens on others, and used the fast to actually manipulate people. The fast was an outward act of religious obedience but had no heart. They attempted to show their spiritual earnestness by enduring minor inconveniences of fasting. Despite this little show of abstinence, they retained their basic lifestyle of disobedience and rebellion against God's moral laws. They were using God's system to get what they wanted. It was a ritualistic fast.

God desired that they would draw near with humility of heart, honest prayer, and submission to His ways. Ritualism is like a painted fire in the fireplace; it cannot warm. A painting of a banquet cannot satisfy hunger. A formal, ritualistic fasting without spiritual content cannot satisfy the heart of God. It accomplishes nothing. It is injurious to the one who fasts and to those around him. It warps judgments, deadens conscience, hardens the heart and awakens false hopes. Fasting must be joined with intercessory prayer out of a clean heart, an honest and humble heart, a heart that is first loving and submissive to a sovereign God.

Prayer that blames or accuses God, as Israel blamed God for taking no notice of their fasting, is not prayer; it is complaining. If our motives reveal any of Israel's blatant flaws in fasting, those of a ritualistic attitude and complaining spirit, let us take to heart the word of honest rebuke.

Right Fasting

Isaiah 58:6-12 describes the fast God loves and responds to. The Lord rewards that which is done right, with right motive and right heart. The right fasting, an act of humility and hope in God, will induce Him to bestow His blessings. Reading Isaiah 58:6-12 encourages the intercessor to combine godly fasting with the prayer of intercession.

"Is this not the fast that I have chosen: to loose the bonds of wickedness, to undo the heavy burdens, to let the oppressed go free, and that you break every yoke? Is it not to share your bread with the hungry, and that you bring to your house the poor who are cast out; when you see the naked, that you cover him, and not hide yourself from your own flesh? Then your light shall break forth like the morning, your healing shall spring forth speedily, and your righteousness shall go before you; the glory of the Lord shall be your rear guard. Then you shall call, and the Lord will answer; you shall cry, and He will say, 'Here I am.' If you take away the yoke from your midst, the pointing of the finger, and speaking wickedness, if you extend your soul to the hungry and satisfy the afflicted soul, then your light shall dawn in the darkness, and your darkness shall be as the noonday. The Lord will guide you continually, and satisfy your soul in drought, and strengthen your bones; you shall be like a watered garden, and like a spring of water, whose waters do not fail. Those from among you shall build the old waste places; you shall raise up the foundations of many generations; and you shall be called the Repairer of the Breach, the Restorer of Streets to Dwell In" (Isaiah 58:6-12).

Goals to Effective Fasting Prayer

Prayer-intercession moves into the breach, the spiritual gap, and begins to pray repentance, restoration, revival and redirection for people—saved and unsaved. This should be the intercessor's prayer while fasting. This is the prayer God desires from fasting intercessors. "Is this not the fast I have chosen?" Combine this spirit of intercession with the fasting of an honest heart, with Isaiah 58:6-12 to guide us, and the result will be powerful prayers with Kingdom results.

To Loose the Bonds of Wickedness

The word "loose" in the Hebrew means "to move with a sudden springing motion, to open a shut door, to set free, to unbind a prisoner, untie the knot in a rope." The target of intercession with fasting is to loose what wickedness has bound, to intercede against those who lawlessly pursue all which is vain and false, in utter disregard of God. The wicked live in reckless surrender to evil passions, in inner clamor, without peace. The wicked are at war and do not know where to turn. They are bound and tied up, every knot guarded by specially assigned demonic powers.

This wickedness is the prayer-target of the fasting intercessor. Keep this picture in mind as prayer is offered. Intercede to loose the bands of wickedness from people, marriages, whole families, neighborhoods, cities and nations. This high calling is fulfilled with prayer-intercession and fasting.

When there is a proper understanding of wickedness, a proper prayer will be offered. Corruption is all around us in today's society. Happiness is defined as gratification of sensual desires. Homosexuality, immorality, adultery, fornication, and pornography are all vices that are increasing rapidly and destroying everyone in their grip. Prayer-intercession confronts this evil, interceding to loose the sexually addicted, to loose the adulterer, to loose the homosexual. When a confused society turns a deaf ear to God and the Church, it is time for intercession with fasting. Society is redefining right and wrong. A new moral pluralism is gaining ground. Traditional immoralities now emerge as new moral alternatives. Crime is soaring, but so is prayer-intercession with fasting. Thousands have answered the call. Millions are being called to fulfill an Isaiah 58 fast that looses the chains of wickedness.

To Undo Heavy Burdens and Let the Oppressed Go Free.

The word "oppression" describes a work of the enemy against individuals or groups. Oppressed means "to press down heavily, to vex, to shatter the emotions or mind, to be crushed and squeezed into a tight place." Prayer-intercession targets the spirit of oppression, sees this as a spiritual battle. Depression, emotional instability, and mental illness can all fall under this category of oppression. We are to intercede for the oppressed that they will be freed and restored to spiritual, emotional and mental health. (See Isaiah 1:17.) Oppression is the work of the devil and we are to destroy his authority over people. (See Acts 10:38.) This will only be accomplished through prayer-intercession with fasting and perseverance. (See Psalms 56:1, 107:39, 119:134; Numbers 10:9; Zephaniah 3:1; Job 35:9.)

To Break Every Yoke

The goal of intercession is to break every evil band or yoke from the oppressed. The yoke was an emblem of servitude; it was a curved piece of wood placed upon the neck of animals or slaves. The yoke was fastened on prisoners who had been captured. They were in bondage, forced to serve their enemies in humiliation and shame. The yoke was held in position by bands or bonds. These were leather straps under the neck of the prisoner. The more bonds, the greater the bondage to the yoke. Some bands were made of iron and never removed.

Prayer-intercession with fasting is to break the yoke, to break the bands and to set the prisoner free. The Scripture speaks of a number of different yokes.

Yoke of Iron

This was put upon a people who broke God's covenant. "Therefore you shall serve your enemies, whom the Lord will send against you, in hunger, in thirst, in nakedness, and in need of everything; and He will put a yoke of iron on your neck until He has destroyed you" (Deuteronomy 28:48).

Yoke of Abusive Authority

This was the bondage over a people from those in power. "Then Jeroboam and the whole assembly of Israel came and spoke to Rehoboam, saying, 'Your father made our yoke heavy; now therefore, lighten the burdensome service of your father, and his heavy yoke which he put on us, and we will serve you . . .' And he (Rehoboam) spoke to them saying, 'My father made your yoke heavy, but I will add to your yoke; my father chastised you with whips, but I will chastise you with scourges!' " (Kings 12:4, 11).

The Yoke of Oppressive Burdens

This speaks of the oppressive laws put on a people. "For You have broken the yoke of his burden and the staff of his shoulder, the rod of his oppressor, as in the day of Midian" (Isaiah 9:4).

The Yoke of Babylonian Control

This is when one nation oppresses and controls another. "I also spoke to Zedekiah king of Judah according to all these words, saying, 'Bring your necks under the yoke of the king of Babylon, and serve him and his people, and live!' " (Jeremiah 27:12).

" 'And I will bring back to this place Jeconiah the son of Jehoiakim, king of Judah, with all the captives of Judah who went to Babylon,' says the Lord, 'for I will break the yoke of the king of Babylon . . .' Then Hananiah the prophet took the yoke off the prophet Jeremiah's neck and broke it." (Jeremiah 28:4,10).

The Yoke of Compulsive Sexual Disorders

This is tormenting millions in our nation. It costs the government (and you and I because we pay taxes) one hundred thousand dollars in medical and welfare benefits for every single teenager who has a child. Last year it cost America 16.6 billion dollars, not counting the cost of four hundred thousand teenage abortions. Pre-marital sex is not only out of control, it is now accepted as a cultural norm. But it is not a norm; it is a yoke, with many bands wrapped around the necks of the immoral.

A compulsion is an irresistible impulse to perform an irrational act. C.S. Lewis in his book, *The Great Divorce*, invents a demonic lizard of lust that has sharp claws that he buries deeply into his victims. As soon as the lizard is thrust through with a sword, the victim is set free from compulsive lustful attitudes. Prayer-intercession is the sword that strikes a deadly blow to the "lizard of lust." Our society is filled with sexually provocative magazines, television ads, sports ads, all containing gross, blatant lies about sex. This lie has mangled many young lives. In Josh McDowell's book, *Why Wait?*, we read the sad testimony of one whom the "lizard of lust" caught and almost destroyed:

Intercession with fasting believes God to shatter these yokes.

> Premarital sex gave me fear as a gift and shame to wear as a garment. It stole my peace of mind and robbed me of hope in a bright future. Sex smashed my concentration in class to smithereens. My desire for church activities was ground to a pulp. It made crumbs of the trust I had known in Christ, and in men and women. Sex gave me a jagged tear in my heart that even now, seven years later, is still healing.[6]

The prayer of intercession attacks the yokes upon people, cities and nations. Intercession with fasting believes God to shatter these yokes. The yoke is destroyed by the power of anointed intercession.

"It shall come to pass in that day His burden will be taken away from your shoulder and his yoke from your neck and the yoke will be destroyed because of the anointing oil" (Isaiah 10:27). (See Leviticus 26:13; Jeremiah 2:20, 5:5.)

Breaking Yokes Through Fasting and Intercession

The breaking of the yoke is possible. It will happen through Spirit-driven prayer, anointed, specific and bold. It will happen through the prayer of the intercessor who believes that the breaker goes before us.

"The breaker will go before them. They will break through, pass in through the gate and go out through it, and their king will pass on before them, the Lord at their head" (Micah 2:13, Amplified Bible).

To break the yoke describes a shattering, a demolishing, a total destruction to the yoke and the bands. (See Romans 8:21; John 8:32, 36.) Our prayer-intercession is clothed in the power of the Holy Spirit. This kind of praying believes that He who is in us is greater than he who is in the world. The New Testament affirms over forty times that our source of power is God. We are to be strong in the power of His might. (See Ephesians 6:10-11; Romans 15:18-19; I Corinthians 1:17-18.)

"And my speech and my preaching were not with persuasive words of human wisdom, but in demonstration of the Spirit and of power, that your faith should not be in the wisdom of men but in the power of God" (I Corinthians 2:4-5). (See I Corinthians 4:20; Ephesians 5:18-20, 3:16-17; I Thessalonians 1:5; Matthew 4:23; Luke 4:36.)

Prayer-intercession with fasting is the only power that will shatter twenty-first century yokes. The yoke of working disorders, even excellent traits, such as willingness to work hard, can become yokes. Hopeless indebtedness is a very real and common yoke in our nation.

When work habits produce workaholics, we come to serve our work as if it is all we have for fulfillment. We put in long hours, not because we have to, but because we want to. It is a driving addiction to work, a compulsion. This yoke destroys marriages, families, health and church life. This addiction to work may become like a drug. This yoke can be identified in people who are unduly critical of others' work habits, have a need to control and a driving desire for recognition and position. A person under this yoke is out of touch with his or her feelings, is physically restless much of the time and becomes easily provoked to anger. This yoke destroys family relationships and family vacations. This yoke ruins friendships. It must be broken off many people. It is a spiritual bondage.

Biblical Purposes of Prayer-Intercession with Fasting

The power of prayer-intercession is a weapon against all forces of evil. Scripture clearly states the biblical purposes for fasting.

- When facing impossible circumstances. (See Nehemiah 12:4; I Samuel 31:13.)
- For repentance, both personally and united with others, for a nation. (See I Samuel 7:6; Nehemiah 9:1; Jonah 3:5.)
- To hear from God (fresh direction). (See Ezra 8:21.)

- To provoke God to move on behalf of others. (See II Chronicles 20:3; Esther 4:16; Daniel 9:3; Job 23:3-5; Isaiah 41:21.)
- To petition the Lord. (See Hebrews 5:7; Acts 10:30.)
- To seek the mind of God. (See Acts 13:2, 14:23.)
- To prepare for ministering in the power and grace of God. (See Matthew 4:2; Acts 13:3.)
- For spiritual power. (See Matthew 17:21; Luke 4:14.)
- To afflict the soul. (See Leviticus 16:29; Psalm 35:13; Proverbs 20:27; I Thessalonians 5:23; Hebrews 4:12.)

Man's state before the Fall was that of a spirit-led man. His spirit had dominion in his life, empowered by God's Spirit. When Adam and Eve sinned, they gave way to their souls and, thus, became soul-led people. Each person born since then has inherited this nature. All of us are controlled by our soulish desires (that of the mind, will and emotions) rather than our spirits, which would cause us to be spiritual people.

Fasting puts the soul back in its place of submission to the spirit by saying "no" to the soulish appetite for food and carnal pleasures.

- The first sin was the result of an uncontrolled appetite. (See Genesis 3.)
- Esau lost his birthright as the result of an uncontrolled appetite. (See Genesis 25:29.)
- One of the sins of Israel was related to the nation's desire for food. (See Numbers 11:5, 33-34.)
- Because of Eli's lack of self-discipline in his eating habits, his own life was affected as well as the lives of his children and the nation. (See I Samuel 4:12-18.)
- We are warned that by not controlling our appetites, we may be led into deception. (See Proverbs 23:1.)
- We are warned not to associate with gluttonous people. (See Proverbs 23:1, 20.)
- Paul buffeted his body to keep it under subjection. (See I Corinthians 9:27.)
- Jesus and Paul put the appetite in proper perspective. (See Luke 12:22; Philippians 3:19; I Corinthians 10:31; Romans 14:17.)

FINAL THOUGHTS ON FASTING

- Fasting deepens humility.
  Ezra 8:21; I Peter 5:6
- Fasting increases hunger for God to work.
- Fasting intensifies prayer concentration.
- Fasting solidifies determination.
- Fasting feeds your faith.
- Fasting opens you more fully to the Spirit's working.
- Fasting fires earnestness and zeal.
- Fasting breaks the strongholds of the appetite.

PRACTICAL SUGGESTIONS

- Fast for a meal occasionally and spend the mealtime (and, if possible, additional time) in prayer.
- Pray about planning for fasting as a regular part of your devotional life.
- Spend the first part of your time feasting on God's word, worshipping, adoring and praising the Lord.
- Be flexible in your fasting. Set a fasting goal rather than being legalistic.
- Do not attempt long fasts (20-40 days) unless you have been informed how to do it.
- Keep a listening ear for the Lord's guidance when He calls you to a special fast for a particular need.
- Keep your fasting a matter between you and God alone.

Further Study

1. What role did fasting play in the Bible? In early church history?

2. What is the difference between wrong fasting and right fasting?

3. What are the purposes of prayer intercession with fasting? What can fasting and prayer accomplish?

4. What are the yokes that can be broken through prayer intercession with fasting? Are there any yokes you need to have broken in your own life?

Notes

1. Paul Yonggi Cho, <u>Prayer–Key to Revival</u> (Word Books, 1984), 113-115.
2. Keil and Delizch, <u>Community on the Old Testament</u> (Grand Rapids, MI: Eerdmans Publishing).
3. Andrew Murray, <u>With Christ in the School of Prayer</u> (Uhrichsville, OH: Barbour Books, 1992).
4. Franklin Hall.
5. Bill Gothard, "Bill Gothard Advanced Leaders' Seminar Notes".
6. Josh McDowell, <u>Why Wait?</u> (Word Publishers).

The Success
Implementing Prayer-Intercession

Chapter Sixteen:
Individual Prayer-Intercession

One year at our youth camp, the counselors felt a deep intercessory burden for the youth. Many teenagers had no apparent spiritual appetite, and some were in open rebellion. Hours of intercession were spent crying out for a breakthrough in their lives. Today those same young people are in the forefront of spiritual activity currently taking place in our church. During that time of crisis, personal intercession over these young people resulted in what we see today—the fruit of young adults with a passion for God and a deep sense of the call of God on their lives.

Every believer has experienced personal prayer burdens for other people. Some burdens arise out of personal relationships with other people, based on specific knowledge of needs. Other prayer burdens arise entirely out of Holy Spirit-directed prayer, without natural knowledge.

This chapter will be directed toward those who have a desire to increase personal intercession for other people. Every believer has the privilege of praying apostolic, New Testament prayers. In Colossians 1:9-12, the Apostle Paul is interceding for the Colossian church. We see this beautiful pastoral side of Paul in many of his epistles, as he offers his continual prayers on behalf of the saints. Here are just a few.

Apostolic Prayers

- "Therefore I also, after I heard of your faith in the Lord Jesus and your love for all the saints, *do not cease to give thanks for you, making mention of you in my prayers*: that the God of our Lord Jesus Christ, the Father of glory, may give to you the spirit of wisdom and revelation in the knowledge of Him, the eyes of your understanding being enlightened; that you may know what is the hope of His calling, what are the riches of the glory of His inheritance in the saints, and what is the exceeding greatness of His power toward us who believe, according to the working of His mighty power which He worked in Christ when He raised Him from the dead and seated Him at His right hand in the heavenly places" (Ephesians 1:15-20).

- "Therefore I ask that you do not lose heart at my tribulations for you, which is your glory. For this reason *I bow my knees to the Father* of our Lord Jesus Christ, from whom the whole family in heaven and earth is named, *that He would grant you*, according to the riches of His glory, to be strengthened with might through His Spirit in the inner man, that Christ may dwell in your hearts through faith; that you, being rooted and grounded in love, may be able to comprehend with all the saints what is the width and length and depth and height–to know the love of Christ which passes knowledge; that you may be filled with all the fullness of God. Now to Him who is able to do exceedingly abundantly above all that we ask or think, according to the power that works in us, to Him be glory in the church by Christ Jesus to all generations, forever and ever. Amen" (Ephesians 3:13-21).

- "Paul, Silvanus, and Timothy, to the church of the Thessalonians in God the Father and the Lord Jesus Christ: grace to you and peace from God our Father and the Lord Jesus Christ. We give thanks to God always for you all, *making mention of you in our prayers*, remembering *without ceasing* your work of faith, labor of love, and patience of hope in our Lord Jesus Christ in the sight of our God and Father" (I Thessalonians 1:1-3).

- "For what thanks can we *render to God for you*, for all the joy with which we rejoice for your sake before our God, *night and day praying exceedingly* that we may see your face and perfect what is lacking in your faith? Now may our God and Father Himself, and our Lord Jesus Christ, direct our way to you. And may the Lord make you increase and abound in love to one another and to all, just as we do to you, so that He may establish your hearts blameless in holiness before our God and Father at the coming of our Lord Jesus Christ with all His saints" (I Thessalonians 3:9-13).

- "*Pray without ceasing*, in everything give thanks; for this is the will of God in Christ Jesus for you. . . . Now may the God of peace Himself sanctify you completely; and may your whole spirit, soul, and body be preserved blameless at the coming of our Lord Jesus Christ. He who calls you is faithful, who also will do it. . . . The grace of our Lord Jesus Christ be with you. Amen" (I Thessalonians 5:17-18, 23-24, 28).

- "We are *bound to thank God always for you*, brethren, as it is fitting, because your faith grows exceedingly, and the love of every one of you all abounds toward each other. . . . Therefore we also *pray always for you* that our God would count you worthy of this calling, and fulfill all the good pleasure of His goodness and the work of faith with power, that the name of our Lord Jesus Christ may be glorified in you, and you in Him, according to the grace of our God and the Lord Jesus Christ" (II Thessalonians 1:3, 11-12).

The Apostle Paul's heart led him into the habit of personal intercession for those with whom he had a spiritual relationship. Paul's habit was to bend his knees, to kneel before the Lord and pray with deep emotion and earnest intensity. Kneeling is one of the prayer postures used by serious praying leaders. (See Daniel 6:10; Mark 10:17, 1:40; I Kings 8:34; Acts 7:60, 9:10, 20:36, 21:5; Luke 22:41.)

A Model of Personal Prayer-Intercession

Paul begins Colossians 1:2-8 with a prayer of thanksgiving, and then in verses 9-12 adds his fervent personal prayer of intercession. It may well be said that Colossians 1:9-12 teaches us more about the essence of personal prayer-intercession than any other New Testament passage. This prayer of intercession shows the fervor of Paul's spirit for the people he loved. No part of this letter is so lofty, so impassioned, so full of his soul as when he moves from speaking *of* God to men to speaking *to* God for men. Here is a model of personal prayer-intercession for all believers to follow. This prayer offers us specific insights of personal intercession.

"For this reason we also, since the day we heard it, do not cease to pray for you, and to ask that you may be filled with the knowledge of His will in all wisdom and spiritual understanding; that you may have a walk worthy of the Lord, fully pleasing Him, being fruitful in every good work and increasing in the knowledge of God; strengthened with all might, according to His glorious power, for all patience and long-suffering with joy; giving thanks to the Father who has qualified us to be partakers of the inheritance of the saints in the light" (Colossians 1:9-12).

Personal intercession is *focused praying*—"for this cause." There is a sense of grace, direction, and petition applied to the specific situation of the people being prayed for. Paul had received some news concerning the Colossian believers. They were in need of certain immediate spiritual elements to balance and complete their Christian character.

Personal intercession is to be a *timeless praying*. "I ceased not" is Paul's testimony. It is a constant and fervent prayer with patience and faith. We may tire quickly of certain people's failures and shortcomings; we may even feel too discouraged to keep praying. We may tire of the immature actions of those we lead, tire of their wrong attitudes, superficial commitments, surface love, carnality and sin. But personal intercession must not tire easily. God Himself will grant us a new heart for the people we love, a new attitude of compassion and grace. This will, most certainly, only happen when we are on our knees, taking them continuously to the throne of God. Cease not!

Personal intercession is *unselfish praying*—"I ceased not to pray for you." Paul, even though he is in prison, centers his attention on the Colossian church's needs, not his own. Pastors and spiritual leaders may find themselves beat down, under attack, busy with church programs, budget matters, a myriad of pressing details, all part of the pressures of leading and making decisions. Could an attitude of "Why doesn't someone pray for me? I have needs too!" sneak in? When you pray, do your prayers only encompass all of your own needs and responsibilities that are preying on your mind, heart and spirit? How long has it been since you prayed for other people by name, fervently lifting their needs, interceding for their spiritual welfare? Unselfish praying is personal intercession.

"And if we know that He hears us, whatever we ask, we know that we have the petitions that we have asked of Him" (I John 5:15).

Colossians 1:9-12 presents specific requests made by Paul. These serve as a pattern for personal intercession. We will examine each part of this model prayer in four personal prayer petitions.

- That you may be filled with the knowledge of God's will.
- That you may be filled with all spiritual wisdom and understanding.
- That you may walk in a manner worthy of the Lord.
- That you may bear fruit in every good work.
- That you may increase in the knowledge of God
- That you may be strengthened with all power.
- That you may patiently endure.
- That you may be filled with joy.

Personal Intercession–First Petition

" . . . that you may be filled with the knowledge of His will" (Colossians 1:9).

To be filled is to be fully equipped, like a ship made ready for a long voyage. It also means "to be controlled by that which you have received." Paul's prayer is that those believers might be "controlled" by the full knowledge of God's will. When the barrel is full of wheat, there is no room for chaff. True knowledge excludes error. There is no room for self to control the believer if the believer is filled to capacity with knowledge of God's will. Prayer-intercession begins by asking that every believer be filled with an ever-growing knowledge of the awesome will of God. Our prayer's chief object is to know His will. (See Colossians 1:19, 25, 2:2, 9-10, 4:12, 17; John 1:16.)

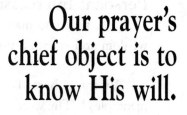

Our prayer's chief object is to know His will.

"The will of God is often enshrouded in darkness, clouded in ambiguity. Silence, as well as speaking, marks His communication with us. In prayer we struggle to discern God's will. We talk. We listen. We ponder Scriptures. We reflect. We wait. And graciously the response comes. Not according to our timetable, nor in the form and mode of our design, but in God's timing and God's way" (*Communicator's Commentary*).

Such knowledge of God's will is the foundation of Christian conduct. The word "knowledge" used here in the Greek is *epignosis*.

- Knowledge in the fullest sense—deep, accurate comprehension.
- Knowledge regarding a definite subject.
- Knowledge which fully grasps and reveals the subject.
- Knowledge, especially the knowledge of God and of Christ, as being the perfection of knowledge.

To be filled with this divine knowledge, divine knowledge, suggests that such knowledge is to pervade all of one's being, thoughts, affections, purposes and plans. It is not possessions and money that Paul prays for specifically, but true knowledge, knowledge of spiritual realities, that knowledge which is the principal thing. Personal petition begins with one question asked most frequently by believers, "What is God's will for me, now, in this situation?" College, marriage, children, promotion, relocation, the purchase of a home . . . in ever area, at every stage, people earnestly desiring to know the will of God, what God intends to do Himself and what He desires us to do. The will of God, in the broadest and most inclusive sense, is the whole purpose of God as revealed in Christ. The will of God is His intention in Christ, in the Church and in our personal lives.

Personal Intercession—Second Petition

" . . . that you may be filled with the knowledge of His will in all wisdom and spiritual understanding" (Colossians 1:9).

"Wisdom," here, is *sophia*, which means "a spiritual grasp of basic principles." The word "understanding" is *sunesis*, or "critical knowledge, the ability to apply basic biblical principles to any given situation that may arise in life."

Personal intercession pleads that the person you pray for may understand the great truths of Scripture and may be able to apply those truths to the tasks and decisions of life. A person may quite easily be a master in theology but a failure in living. People may be able to talk about eternal truths yet be helpless to apply them to areas of their lives.

Personal intercession prays that Ephesians 1:17-18 becomes a reality: "That the Father of glory may give you the spirit of wisdom and revelation in the knowledge of Him, the eyes of your understanding being enlightened." The spirit of wisdom is insight into the deeper things of God. The spirit of revelation provides insights and discernment from the Spirit about divine truth and divine will.

Personal Intercession–Third Petition

" . . . that you may walk in a manner worthy of the Lord, fully pleasing Him, being fruitful in every good work" (Colossians 1:9).

The Colossians were attracted to deeper truths, deeper knowledge and deeper spiritual revelation, yet these things were unconnected with the way they lived. They separated learning from living, knowledge from obedience, prayer from practice.

Our intercession for those we love is that their lives be based on spiritual truth, not to compromise through misuse of spiritual truths or spiritual experiences. The end of all prayers is obedience to truth, a desire that our lives be shaped by the Spirit. The result of spiritual intercession for others should be a deepening of their Christian character. To live a life worthy of the Lord comes from knowledge of His divine will. As D.L. Moody once said, "Every Bible should be bound in shoe leather." The end of all knowledge is godly conduct, not mystical philosophy. The error of the Colossians, and of each of us today, is that Christianity was merely a system of truth to be believed instead of embraced and lived out. In all of us, the flesh prevents the perfect translation of knowledge into conduct that is pleasing to the Lord. As we make personal intercession for those we love, we name these areas and pray specifically, "Thy will be revealed." If you are interceding for a person you know well, you may name the sins that are preventing a walk worthy of the Lord's blessings. (See Exodus 31:3; Deuteronomy 4:6; I Corinthians 1:19; Ephesians 4:1; Philippians 1:27-28; I Thessalonians 2:12, 4:1; Colossians 2:6, 3:7, 4:4.)

When interceding for those we love, prayer should include four areas.

• *Pray for their spiritual desires.* What do they deeply desire? Do they need to return to a first-love relationship with the Lord? Have they set their affections on the wrong things? The Holy Spirit is able to change the desires of our hearts. Begin to list the affections that Scripture teaches we are to have. Proclaim these over them daily, specifically.

- *Pray for direction in their spiritual lives.* What do they seek after? Are they confused, discouraged, heading in the wrong direction, refusing godly counsel? To walk in a manner worthy of the Lord's blessings, they must walk according to the principles of God's word. Pray for the divine pressure of the Holy Spirit to guide them toward the Lord's will and direction for their lives. What attitudes prevent them from having a humble or a teachable spirit? Pray for their wills to be in unity with the Lord's will, for their thinking to be open to the Lord's thoughts and His clear leading.

- **Pray that they will be fruitful in every good work as they walk with the Lord.** "To walk" is *peripateo* in the Greek. It is "to live a life with obvious outward expressions of a deep inward work of grace." "To bear fruit" is in the present tense in the Greek, meaning "a continual fruitfulness because of a continual supply of grace and strength from the Holy Spirit." We may, with natural eyes, see only a lack of fruit-bearing. Our intercession is to focus on the great potential for fruit-bearing by God's supernatural strength. (See Ephesians 2:10; Galatians 5:5; Titus 1:16, 2:7,14, 3:8, 3:15.)

- **Pray that they will increase in the knowledge of God.** To walk in a manner that is worthy of God's blessings, one must walk in the basic principles that invoke those blessings. Pray that the ones you are interceding for will have a new hunger and a strong desire for more of God's rich knowledge. Pray spiritual enlargement for them. With true, personal knowledge of God, spiritual growth occurs.

Personal Intercession–Fourth Petition
" . . . strengthened with all might according to His glorious power for all patience and long-suffering with joy . . ." (Colossians 1:11).

"Being made powerful in all power according to the might of His glory for all perseverance and long-suffering with joy. The point here is to bring the working power of God out of the past and into the present. Christ is our present power, now, here, today, in this present moment" (*Lenski Commentary*).

Ephesians 1:19 also reads, "And what is the exceeding greatness of His power toward us who believe, according to the working of His mighty power." This mighty power is available now for every believer. (See Ephesians 2:16; Romans 7:21; II Corinthians 4:11.)

Why is it that we continue in our anemic life, feebly getting on as best we can? Why is it that we plod along, our Christian walk a mere stumble rather than a stride? Why is it that we give way to petty defects and become uninspiring spectacles of spiritual ineffectiveness? Why do we allow mean carnality to shape our lives? According to this prayer of Paul, we can remedy this state with God's supernatural power that strengthens us beyond our human frailties. This word "strengthen," used in Paul's prayer, speaks of continuous empowerment and is translated from the same root Greek word as is found in Philippians 4:13: "I can do all things through Him who gives me strength."

This is a constant renewal for our constant need. This is the continuous process of God's bestowing and our receiving of His might, a process rendered necessary by our continual human weakness and the wear and tear of life. This power comes from God's glorious might. It is not proportioned simply to meet our needs, but proportioned according to God's abundant supply. Infinite spiritual riches await us, even while we are in our narrow rooms. As we intercede for individuals, we pray release of the great power of God into their lives, their homes, their businesses, their crises. The infinite strength of God will renew the marital, physical, spiritual, financial and emotional circumstances of the ones for whom we intercede. As we pray, let us lift our voices with confidence in the power of God to accomplish even more than we can ask or think. God's energy is ready to be released and is waiting for our petition. Our prayer is for the power of God to be made manifest.

Intercession Faith Targets

- Pray for the power of God to fill the whole life of the people interceded for, with a new release of God's glorious might, now, today, into their worlds. We believe and pray that God's power will transform them, enable them to overcome all their problems, limitations and weaknesses.

- Pray for the Spirit of God to encourage and strengthen those for whom you intercede. Rebuke the spirit or attitude of discouragement. Pray for a spirit of endurance that refuses to be daunted by hard times. Pray against cowardice and despondency, but for boldness and joy. Pray for their capacity to see things through to the end, all the way through, without quitting. There are difficulties that believers undergo for which this is no avenue of relief or release. We need to pray that they will have the power to endure. Pray God's promises. In every situation God will grant grace and power to enable them to endure and to make it through.

- Pray for the perfect attitude of patience, the refusal to be upset by difficult, irritating, offensive people. The attitude of true godly patience is of the utmost importance for all growing believers. This is the opposite of wrath or a spirit of revenge. This is an attitude that refuses to retaliate, no matter what injury or insult is suffered.

We may live and work with people who try to provoke us, spitefully use us and scorn us. Some do so deliberately, others unconsciously. We may encounter people who are oblivious to our feelings, callous to our needs, demanding without themselves giving. We need godly patience in all relationships. We need the spiritual power and strength of the Holy Spirit, available through prayer-intercession, to endure rejection and injury. Through prayer-intercession, we enlarge our spirits to receive the great power and grace of God which enables us to keep on loving, forgiving, accepting, long after all human capacity to endure is spent and all natural juices of goodwill are drained from our souls. (See Philippians 2:17, 3:1; Galatians 5:22.)

Further Study

1. What kind of praying is personal intercession?

2. Read Colossians 1:9-12. What are the four petitions in this scripture? How can they serve as a pattern for personal intercession?

3. What does it mean to be filled with the knowledge of His will?

4. When praying for those we love, how should we pray?

Chapter Seventeen:
Corporate Prayer–Intercession

The atmosphere in the sanctuary was electrified with expectation. What would cause such a stirring in the congregation? A visiting ministry with an unusual gift of healing? A well known national singer or singing group? No, this was not the case at all. It was a special night of corporate, all church prayer. The sanctuary was nearly full on Sunday night . . . just for prayer?

This was not an ordinary prayer time, but a night of corporate cleansing through repentance and confession. There were two trashcans placed near the altar into which church members would put thousands of pieces of paper with confessed sins, brokenness and declarations of victory. The service began with the reading of Scripture, and then everyone was asked to assume a postrate position on the floor.

What an unusual sight! Twenty-five hundred people lying on the floor! This is a corporate prayer meeting. The power released when the whole church prays is absolutely mind-boggling. God is restoring corporate church intercession as a function of the main church service for every believer.

The prayer of intercession seeks to stand in the gap, rebuild spiritual hedges, fill the prayer cup in heaven and reclaim spiritual borders. Prayer-intercession engages in strategic levels of spiritual warfare. The warfare against the mind of the intercessor is continuous and strategic. Ephesians 6:10-17 depicts the intercessor's battlefield. We do not war against flesh and blood but against principalities and powers, spiritual wickedness in high places. This level of warfare is fought by both the individual believer and, at times, the corporate church, the whole of the local body of Christ. The importance of the whole church praying together at one time is underscored in Scripture.

Biblical Models of Corporate Intercession

Corporate intercession is modeled throughout the Bible in both the Old and New Testaments. (See I Chronicles 16:11; Genesis 4:26; Judges 3:9; 6:6-9; 10:12; II Chronicles 18:31; Ezra 8:21-23; Acts 12:4-5, 1:15, 4:31.)

...prayer intercession has the power to ruin Satan's worst strategies.

There are certain challenges in the spirit realm that can only be accomplished through corporate intercession. Corporate intercession, as seen in Scripture and throughout history, should be a normal, powerful functioning part of our church services. Prayer-intercession should not be relegated to the usually not-so-well-attended meetings. If prayer-intercession has the power to ruin Satan's worst strategies–to destroy his principalities and powers regionally, bring national revival, heal the land and release the supernatural–surely it must be an integral and important part of our corporate gatherings. Intercession is for all believers, the whole Church, men, women, teenagers, children. Isaiah 56:7 states that God's desire is to build a *house* of prayer, not just a room of prayer, but a house.

"And He said to them, 'It is written, "My house shall be called a house of prayer," but you have made it a "den of thieves." ' Then the blind and the lame came to Him in the temple, and He healed them" (Matthew 21:13-14).

The Dangers of Lacking Corporate Intercession

God's purpose will be revealed as the whole Church cooperates. "My house" is God's description of His Church, a house of prayer-intercession. When believers gather together in the House of God–the Church–a spiritual explosion of faith, prayer and worship should occur. Many matters that consume our energies seem very important to us at times, but in the long run, most prove to be meaningless. They have little or no eternal consequence. These unimportant matters drain our time, energy and resources, all of which should be applied to eternal matters and to prayer-intercession.

Millions of dollars and countless volunteer hours are expended seeking inventive ways to draw the world into the Church. Hundreds of books are written and published each year, advising the Church how to reach the world. Ideas. Methods. Creativity. Drama. Shorter preaching. Relevant preaching. Contemporary music. Felt-need ministry. This list could go on for a very long time. The problem is that most churches are not growing, are not spiritually healthy, are not spiritually powerful. Why? The main thing has not stayed the main thing! The most valuable and powerful growth tool has been stored away, put in an old shed out back and forgotten. Even the majority of churches that do pray today know little about prevailing prayers of deep supplication and intercession.

We have learned from the Korean church how corporate prayer affects the growth of the Church. Of the twenty churches in the world that count a weekend attendance of twenty thousand or more, nine of them are in Korea. The largest Baptist church, the largest Methodist church, the largest Presbyterian church, the largest Holiness church and the largest Pentecostal church in the world are all in Korea.[1] Korea's church leaders say that fasting and corporate prayer-intercession is the key. The Korean churches have established the following strong habits of corporate prayer:

Early Morning Prayer. All around Korea, 365 days a year, thousands of believers pray every morning from four o'clock until five o'clock in the morning and from five o'clock until six o'clock in the evening.

Friday All-Night Prayer Meetings. In almost all Korean churches, these meetings are scheduled from ten o'clock Friday evening until dawn Saturday morning. Given the fact that there are seven thousand churches in Seoul, Korea, there could be as many as two hundred fifty thousand believers praying all night in that one city alone!

The failure of the church today is the failure to engage in prayer-intercession.

Prayer Mountains. In Korea, prayer mountains are common. At last count more than two hundred churches had one. Thousands upon thousands retreat to these mountains for intense prayer and fasting.[2] And we wonder why our churches in America are not growing through conversion alone?

The failure of the Church today is the failure to engage in prayer-intercession. The motor of this great ship called "the Church" is corporate prayer. When the Church gathers, she should pray together, in one accord, with one voice. When we, as God's people, elevate and return prayer-intercession to its rightful place, the Church will function as it is built to, with grace and power. Prayer is the power that unlocks the door of God's treasure house. The power of corporate prayer is influenced by the power in every individual believer's prayer life. Every believer should be encouraged, equipped and inspired to grow in prayer-intercession. This can be accomplished many ways: teaching, discipling, holding seminars, etc. Additionally, the corporate prayer life can be and should be a mighty influence on the believer's personal payer life. The Church's ultimate effectiveness will be determined by its corporate prayer life. Therefore let us make a commitment right now to join with our churches in corporate prayer-intercession. (See II Chronicles 15:12.)

"If My people who are called by My name will humble themselves, and pray and seek My face, and turn from their wicked ways, then I will hear from heaven, and will forgive their sin and heal their land" (II Chronicles 7:14).

Following the Book of Acts Intercession Model

A quick survey of the book of Acts reveals the first church of the first century, the church Christ founded, was a praying church. The book of Acts, called "the Acts of the Holy Spirit through the Apostles," is saturated with prayer. The first church was a church militant, a church living on her knees! Her witness was dynamic, and her prevailing prayer conquered even the proud legions of Rome.

Satan dreads nothing but prayer.

The old preacher of the past, Samuel Chadwick, stated, "Satan dreads nothing but prayer. The church that lost its Christ was full of good works. The one concern of the devil is to keep the saints from praying. He laughs at our toil, mocks at our wisdom, but trembles when we pray."

Our call is to follow the first church, a church committed to prayer. It would be profitable for us to point out the prayer habits of the first church.

- *Prayer in the Upper Room.* One hundred twenty believers spent ten days in prayer. The church was birthed in prayer and maintained in prayer. (See Acts 1:13-14.)
- *Prayer for Choosing the Right Leadership.* Luke records the

last reference to the casting of lots in the Bible. Prayer was for choosing a successor for Judas. (See Acts 1:24.)

- **Prayer Habits Observed.** The early church had three recognized hours of prayer: the third hour, the sixth hour and the ninth hour of the day. (See Acts 3:1, 2:15, 10:9, 3:1, 10:36; 22:17; Luke 24:53.)
- **Praying Together in One Accord.** They lifted up their voices to God in one accord, asking, "Grant thy servants with all boldness . . ." Through prayer, the church was on the offense, not the defense. (See Acts 4:23, 31.)
- **Prayer a Priority in Ministry.** The apostolic order of leading was prayer first. Their first priority was to give themselves continually to prayer. They were men of prayer, first and foremost. (See Acts 6:4-7.)
- **Prayer of Stephen.** Even as he was dying, Stephen was calling out to God in prayer. (See Acts 7:55-60.)
- **Prayer for Impartation of the Baptism of the Holy Spirit.** Persecution scattered the church, and the blood of the first martyr became the seed of the church. (See Acts 8:14-15, 22, 24-25.)
- **Prayer of Paul At and After Conversion.** Paul had been a praying man all of his life, but it was not until he was born anew by the Spirit that he understood prayer as God sees it. (See Acts 9:5-6,11, 22:8-18, 26:12-19.)
- **Prayer of Faith.** The posture of prayer is one that recognizes our dependence on God. That is why Peter knelt in prayer. (See Acts 9:36-43.)
- **Prayer of Cornelius: A Household Hungry for God.** At the ninth hour of the day, Cornelius was on his knees, crying out to God, when an angel appeared to him in a vision. "Cornelius, your prayers and your alms have come up before God." But it was at the sixth hour of the day that Peter was having his rooftop discussion with God about what is clean and unclean. Three hours before Cornelius asked, God was answering!
- **Prayer Made Without Ceasing.** Peter was in jail, probably about to be killed. So the church went to continuous prayer, prayer without ceasing. Yet when the answer came, the response of those praying was the same as ours often is, "Impossible. It's too good to be true. It can't be!" But it is.
- **Prayer Before Sending Out Ministry Teams.** When the first church wanted to send out a ministry team, it followed a very simple format. Believers ministered to the Lord; they fasted. The Holy Ghost answered; they fasted and prayed; they laid hands and sent out the team. (See Acts 13:2-3, 43.)
- **Prayer and Fasting to Ordain the Elders.** Before ordaining elders, they prayed with fasting. (See Acts 14:23.)

- *Prayer Meeting of Women.* The women had a set time: the Sabbath. They had a set place: by the river. They had a set purpose: to pray. (See Acts 16:13-16.)
- *Prayer in Crisis.* It was midnight and Paul and Silas were locked in chains in prison. Instead of simply praying a crisis prayer of "Oh God, why?" they prayed and then lifted up their voices and sang praises to their God. (See Acts 16:25, 34.)
- *Prayer of Paul at His Farewell.* It was a sad farewell to his elders as they stood on the sands of Miletus. The Ephesian elders had traveled thirty miles to say good-bye to Paul. He bid them farewell with prayer. (See Acts 20:36, 21:5.)

The Power of Corporate Prayer

In Acts 4:31 we read about the power of corporate prayer in the first church and for the Church today. "And when they had prayed, the place where they were assembled together was shaken; and they were all filled with the Holy Spirit, and they spoke the word of God with boldness."

Let us delve into this verse a little more so as not to miss any of its rich content.

- **When they had prayed.** This was not a solo operation. The whole church gathered together with a desire to pray. Every believer had a sense of responsibility, a sense of ownership in the crisis. "When they prayed" speaks of a corporate meeting with corporate or whole church involvement.

- **The place where they were assembled together was shaken.** As church members prayed together in one accord with the lifting of their voices, the power of God was revealed. The power of corporate intercession can cause a shaking, both in the natural and spiritual realms.

- **And they were all filled with the Spirit.** Corporate prayer has the potential of refreshing and refueling the people of God with the Holy Spirit. "They were *all* filled with the Holy Spirit." Undoubtedly there were different levels of maturity represented in this group. Some were very focused and faith-filled in prayer; others might have been discouraged, feeling carnal, not so faith-filled. Yet when prayer was offered together in one place with one voice, they were all filled with the Spirit. Corporate intercession has the power to affect the Church by the Spirit, quickly, deeply and supernaturally.

• *And they spoke the word with boldness.* After this corporate prayer-intercession and the receiving of a supernatural abundance of the Holy Spirit by every believer, boldness was the result. What does the Church today need a great dose of? Boldness to do the work of the Kingdom of God.

Corporate intercession involving the whole church assembled together calls for raising our voices to God. We must pray boldly, even loudly. We must break the bondage of silence in our corporate prayer times. Lifting our voices, crying aloud, speaking forcefully are all biblical descriptions of corporate intercession. (See Psalms 25:1, 32:3, 94:17, 115:17, 143:8; Isaiah 37:4, 40:4, 58:1, 8; Jeremiah 7:16, 11:14, 51:15; Ezekiel 21:22.)

At Paul Yonggi Cho's church in Korea, estimated to be one of the world's largest churches, Pastor Cho describes their corporate intercession. "One of the most important ministries of the Full Gospel Central Church is the prayer in unison we have during every service. We always open our services with everyone present praying together at the same time. We pray for the salvation . . . of our nation. . . . We also pray for our leaders. . . . We pray in unison for the thousands of requests that come to us. . . . We especially pray for a worldwide revival. When I hear my people praying, it sounds like a forceful roar of a mighty waterfall. We know God must hear the sincerity of our prayer because we are praying in unison and unity. As we pray together the power of God is manifested in our midst. Many have been healed, delivered and filled with the Holy Spirit as we have united in prayer."

> Every time we meet together we must let prayer-intercession have its share of time.

Would it be not marvelous to hear the roar of a forceful waterfall in our churches today, the mighty sound of corporate prayer-intercession? Every time we meet together for worship and the word, we must let prayer-intercession have its share of time.

Corporate Intercession Suggestions

Corporate prayer-intercession can take place several different ways. Let me share with you just a few ways we may seek to fulfill this great ministry of prayer.

At the Beginning of the Church Service

In some churches this is called "pre-service prayer." Others call it "opening intercession" or "preparatory praying." Whatever the name, the function is similar. The whole church is called to a time of leadership-led prayer. This can happen easily as the church gathers. At the normal starting time, one chorus can be sung, and then the church moves into unified corporate prayer-intercession. If this is done with wise and sensitive leadership, even the visitor, the new covert, or the spiritually cold saint will enter in.

Since we, as the people of God, may come to corporate worship services unprepared to hear from God, unprepared to minister unto God and unprepared to minister to others, opening service intercession is not optional. We may come with busy minds and busy lives, we need a time to stop and draw our spiritual breath, to calm our spirits and renew our minds so that the worship experience will be far more beneficial, enriched by our preparation.

We, as the priests of the New Testament, must learn to approach God with respect. In the Old Testament, God gave instructions for the proper steps to enter His holy presence. Ignoring or violating these principles causes us to forfeit the rich power of His presence that should be available to us as royal priests. (See I Peter 2:5-9.) Because His instructions were ignored, God rejected Cain's offering. (See Genesis 4:3-4.) God sent His holy fire out from His presence and consumed Nadab and Abihu for their strange offering and improper approach. (See Leviticus 10:1-3.) God struck King Uzziah on the forehead with leprosy for his violation. (See II Chronicles 26:16-21.)

The question is asked in Psalm 24:3-6, "Who may ascend into the hill of the LORD? Or who may stand in His holy place?" The answer is, he who has cleansed his heart, hands and mouth. In Hebrews 10:19-22, we are exhorted to enter into the Holiest place with a sincere heart, full of faith, cleansed of an evil conscience. There is a principle of preparation when approaching the presence of God together as the people of God, Christ's Church. Jacob commanded his household to be clean, to change their garments and to remove all their idols. (See Genesis 35:2-3.)

The Tabernacle of Moses offers a simple, yet powerful, model for approaching the presence of God and can be used as the pattern for corporate service intercession.

Approaching the Presence of God

The Tabernacle Of Moses

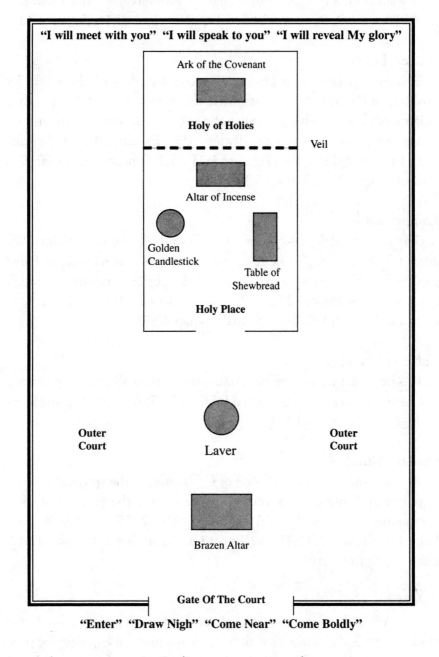

As royal priests, we enter God's presence prepared.

Brazen Altar.

The first element that the priests passed by was the brazen altar. It symbolizes the removal of guilt through confession of sin, and the renewal of the covenant of grace that guarantees forgiveness and cleansing. (See I John 1:6-9; Revelation 1:5, 7:14, 22:14; Ezekiel 44:23; James 4:8.)

Brazen Laver

The brazen laver is a place to remove the dust of the world by washing our minds and spirits with the water of God's word, thus judging ourselves. This is a stage of personal and spiritual inventory, seeing ourselves the way we really are. (See Exodus 30:18; Ephesians 5:26; Isaiah 4:4; I Peter 4:17; James 1:23-25; I Timothy 2:8; Isaiah 6:5; II Corinthians 3:18; Titus 3:5.)

Lampstand

The lampstand represents receiving fresh oil of the Holy Spirit. We allow Christ, our High Priest, to trim our wicks and remove all burnt parts in order to release a new powerful flow of His anointing through our lives. (See Exodus 27:21, 30:7-8; Leviticus 24:3; Ecclesiastes 10:1; Matthew 25:1-13; Ephesians 5:18-19; Isaiah 40:31.)

Table of Shewbread

It is here that we receive personal, spiritual nourishment by partaking of Christ, the Living Bread. (See John 6:27-35, 6:48-52; I Corinthians 10:16-21; Matthew 6:11.)

Golden Altar

As we stand before the throne of God, offering the spiritual incense of prayer and intercession unto Him, we receive the power to live as conquerors. (See Exodus 30:7-8; Psalms 141:1-2, 55:17; Malachi 1:11; Luke 1:6-17; Acts 2:42; Ephesians 6:18; Colossians 4:2; Romans 12:12; Luke 19:46; Revelation 8:2-6.)

Ark of the Covenant

The Ark of the Covenant is the place where God's presence dwells, the place where God communes with man. It is a place of enjoying the presence of God with freedom of spirit. It is a place to worship God with zeal and to be filled with His presence. His presence brings mercy, holiness, reconciliation, communion, the glory of God. (See Psalms 100:4, 22:3; Exodus 29:24-26, 30:36, 40:33-38; Numbers 7:89; II Samuel 6:12-18; Isaiah 6:7-13; I Chronicles 16:4.)

Opening services with intercession prepares the church to enter into Holy Spirit-empowered worship, to receive the word into good soil. This prayer time prepares our hearts. Opening-service intercession leads people into prayer that their own hearts and minds be cleansed from the sins of yesterday and today, from any habits that cause grief to the Holy Spirit. Pray specifically for the blood of Jesus to be released and forgiveness to take place immediately. (See I John 1:1-8; James 4:8; Psalm 24:1-7.)

Opening-service intercession prays specifically for the enemy of our souls to be defeated in every person present in the prayer service and those coming into the services that weekend. This is a time to pray spiritual deliverance for those suffering from spiritual bondages, deception and oppression, the church agreeing in one accord, with one heart and one spirit. The gates of hell cannot withstand the interceding church. (See Isaiah 43:5-7; Matthew 16:16-18.)

In opening-service prayer, intercession is made for families, unsaved husbands, backsliders spouses, abused children, those on the brink of divorce, teenagers searching for help, the lonely single parents and widows. (See I Timothy 2:1.)

Opening-service prayer-intercession may take place on our knees, as the prayer leader directs our praying. It includes people praying together, also, and this may take place by praying in small groups of pray-ers, men with men and women with women or mixed groups, or in standing individually to pray in one accord.

The gates of hell cannot withstand the interceeding church.

Pray for a powerful, evident presence of the Holy Spirit to be upon the worship and the preaching of the Word. Pray for the preacher to have fresh illumination and penetrating power as the Word is preached. Pray for those unsaved in the services to be ready to hear the gospel and to open their hearts to receive Christ.

Opening-service prayer-intercession should be Holy Spirit-led and relevant to the church, the city, the region and the nation. This prayer time may last fifteen, thirty or up to forty-five minutes. Obviously this depends on the needs of the hour.

Corporate Prayer-Intercession Prayer and Praise Service

Another approach to corporate prayer-intercession is what I call a "Prayer and Praise" service (see Appendix for author's example). All of the truth that the Body of Christ receives must be observed. We do this with almost all major, foundational doctrines that we adhere to, such as salvation, water baptism, the Lord's table, worship, giving, etc. Each truth is reviewed and reestablished often, some at almost every corporate church gathering. When corporate prayer-intercession is established through teaching of the Word, the people of God have only received the seed. Some leaders and churches stop too soon, stopping after the soil has been prepared and the seed deposited. The seed of truth must receive the water that will cause the seed to grow. The watering of this seed can be a "Prayer and Praise" service in which the entire service is focused on prayer-intercession.

The order of the service can be changed in order to facilitate this prayer focus. Let me share our church "Prayer and Praise Sunday" approach, hoping this will not only inspire, but will also give you a general order to follow. Obviously, you can follow as closely or loosely as you desire in your particular setting.

First, the order of service could look something like this: an opening song, followed by a short time of prayer-intercession, as presented in the appendix. Then, a chorus or hymn leads into a fifteen-to-twenty minute exhortation/teaching by the pastor or a designated speaker. A large portion of Scripture reading should be included in this exhortation and a definite theme presented, such as the lordship of Christ, benefits of the cross, cleansing, repentance, harvest of the nations, worship with a pure heart, new love for God, prayer, intercession, family altar, etc. All of these themes are applied to the individual through prayer. Prayer is the channel.

The church may read in unison certain Scriptures that have been prepared in advance, using a hand-out or overhead of some type. There may be pre-appointed pray-ers that lead in prayer at certain intervals during the prayer-intercession. Singing at various times during the prayer time causes prayer to be mixed with thanksgiving. After the theme has been covered, end the service with an extended time of praise and worship.

Corporate Prayer-Intercession with Fasting

Calling of the whole church to pray and intercede, united with fasting, is another way to accomplish corporate prayer-intercession. Our church commits to a forty-day fast two or three times a year. It has been quite successful and is easily organized.

We choose a forty-day period, usually at a strategic time such as the beginning of the year (January/February) or before a harvest thrust or in the fall when the people are returning from vacations, school has started and everyone is ready to focus. The forty-day period of prayer and fasting is announced in a bulletin insert far enough in advance to allow everyone to choose which days they will fast. As the forty days fill up with fasting commitments, there is a kick-off Sunday to begin the corporate prayer-intercession. We will, at this point, present a possible intercession agenda of specific areas we want to intercede for. We, thus, accumulate three to four thousand days of fasting by the corporate church during this forty-day fast.

Further Study

1. What are the dangers of not engaging in corporate intercession?

2. What can we learn about corporate intercession from the book of Acts?

3. Read Acts 4:31. What does this verse teach us about the power of corporate prayer?

4. What is the purpose of corporate intercession at the opening of a church service? How can opening service intercession prepare the church for the ministry of God's word and the work of the Holy Spirit?

Notes

1.   Peter Wagner, <u>Churches That Pray</u> (Ventura, CA: Regal Books, 1996), 23.
2.   Peter Wagner, <u>Churches That Pray</u> (Ventura, CA: Regal Books, 1996), 24-26.

Chapter Eighteen:
Making an Intercessory Prayer Covenant

In October of 1982, a twenty-five-year old woman finished the New York City marathon. No big deal, except that Linda Down has cerebral palsy and was the first woman ever to complete the 26.2-mile race on crutches! Although she fell half a dozen times, she kept going until she crossed the finish line, eleven hours after she started. Her disability limited her speed, but not her determination. Henry Wadsworth Longfellow once wrote, "Great the art of beginning, but greater the art of ending."

We have a prayer marathon ahead of us, not a short relay race. Prayer-intercession requires a determination to make it a life habit, a life discipline. Even if we feel like we are running on crutches, our prayer life must continue. We are called to become life-long prayer intercessors, ever learning, applying, changing and moving ahead in the school of prayer.

Igor Gorin, the noted Ukrainian-American baritone, told of his younger days studying voice. He loved to smoke a pipe, but one day his professor said, "Igor, you will have to make up your mind whether you are going to be a great singer or a great pipe smoker. You cannot be both." So the pipe went.

What must you give up to become a great prayer-intercessor?

Do you desire to be a great prayer-intercessor? An average intercessor? Below average? Will you accept failure? What level do you desire to attain in the school of prayer? What must you give up in your lifestyle in order to become a great prayer-intercessor? What will you say "no" to? The ancient Chinese philosopher Mencius said, "Men must first decide what they will not do, and then they are able to act with vision in what they ought to do." The life of prayer will only be developed in the life of discipline. Discipline means choice. Choices determine destiny.

We have journeyed together through many stories, illustrations, and Scriptures on intercessory prayer. Now is the time for our response. Prayer deserves our best commitment. This might involve changing the daily routine–perhaps something as simple as skipping a favorite television show, or going to bed early so we can start the next day early with prayer-intercession. It might mean giving up or modifying a time-consuming hobby. One of the first steps to a better, richer, more powerful prayer life is personal discipline. We must get past the thought that intercessory prayer is a drudgery and see it as a delight.

Do not try to browbeat yourself into a new lifestyle of prayer, or browbeat yourself when your discipline slips. Remember the grace of God. Remember the Holy Spirit desires that you learn to pray, and the Holy Spirit is both our motivator and our enabler. True spiritual discipline achieves a balance of producing but not forcing, of maintaining diligence but not striving.

Let us fix our eyes on the prize: to pray like Jesus prays, intercede like Jesus intercedes, that we may see results in our prayer lives like Jesus had and has. We will not focus on our bad habits or our past failures. Many people's downfalls come in trying to change a bad habit by focusing on an undesirable behavior instead of on the new behavior to replace it. Let us focus on our ability to respond to the Holy Spirit and to His corrections and directions.

Remember, motivation does not come first; action does! We must prime our pump by immediate steps of action, as small as they may be. Action creates motivation. If we wait until we are in the mood, we may wait forever! Prayer discipline is habit forming; a little leads to more because the benefits prove increasingly desirable. Prayer warriors are by definition motivated–having a mission, a passionate commitment to the calling to pray. To move into and sustain a new life of intercessory prayer, we must make a covenant with God, a commitment empowered by Christ's grace and strength.

The Asa Prayer Covenant

We need to make the Asa-covenant found in II Chronicles 15:1-15. Asa was the third king of Judah and the great grandson of King Solomon. He ruled Judah for forty years. The Asa-covenant of prayer has definite, God-given promises for the committed intercessor. "The LORD is with you while you are with Him. If you seek Him, He will be found by you; but if you forsake Him, He will forsake you" (I Chronicles 15:2). (See Deuteronomy 4:29-30; I Chronicles 16:10-11, 22:19, 28:9; II Chronicles 7:14; Psalms 27:4-8, 34:10.)

Asa and all of Judah entered into a covenant to seek the Lord. The word "covenant" carries with it the idea of mutual understanding between two parties, each binding itself to fulfill obligations. It is a legal contract, a binding agreement. The people of Judah entered into this covenant willingly and joyfully, making an oath, which means they swore and obligated themselves, committing themselves with a vow. (See Joel 1:14, 2:12,15; Ezra 8:21-23; I Chronicles 15:14-15.)

"Then Moses spoke to the heads of the tribes concerning the children of Israel, saying, 'This is the thing which the LORD has commanded: if a man vows a vow to the LORD, or swears an oath to bind himself by some agreement, he shall not break his word; he shall do according to all that proceeds out of his mouth' " (Numbers 30:1-2).

This covenant was used to describe a vow made with blood–the strongest type of commitment possible for the people to enter into. Asa was so committed to this covenant that he put to death any and all who would not seek the Lord. (See Deuteronomy 23:21; Ecclesiastes 5:4; Psalms 50:14, 76:11.)

When they entered into this prayer covenant with the oath, they did so with loud voices, shouting and blowing trumpets and rams horns. (See I Chronicles 15:14.) This was a very public occasion. There was no secret oath, no secret commitment, no chance of backing out later. They went for it. They put it all on the line. This prayer covenant caused the people to rejoice, and they sought the Lord with all their hearts, and the Lord was found by them.

It is time for an Asa-prayer-covenant.

Entering the School of Prayer

Prayer is a trade to be learned. We must be apprenticed and serve our time at it. Painstaking care, much thought, practice and labor are required to be a skilled tradesman in praying. Practice makes perfect, in prayer, as in everything. Toiling hands and hearts make professionals in this heavenly trade. Are you ready to become a skilled prayer warrior?

We must start today. Now is the time!

Andrew Murray, in his book, *With Christ in the School of Prayer*, states "May God open our eyes to see what the holy ministry of intercession is to which, as his royal priesthood, we have been set apart. May he give us a large and strong heart to believe what mighty influence our prayers can exert. And may all fear, as to our being able to fulfill our vocation, vanish as we see Jesus, living everyday to pray, living in us to pray, and standing surety for our prayer life."

We must not procrastinate. We must start today. Now is the time to exert mighty influence through prayer-intercession. In 1957, eighty members founded the *Procrastinator's Club of America*, devoted to putting off just about everything until tomorrow or later. None of the eighty members paid dues on time. If they did, they would be thrown out of the club. We must never join this club if we intend to fulfill the call to intercessory prayer. No more can we afford to put off intercessory prayer until tomorrow. We need to enroll today in the school of prayer. Let us pay the tuition and begin.

Establish a time for prayer.

The prayer student's first step is to make a daily appointment with God. This could be even just a few minutes to begin with, increasing as he or she learns more about prayer. Some excellent books advocate early morning praying, and there are some solid reasons that early-morning prayer is beneficial. The Psalms are filled with early-morning prayer Scriptures.

"My voice You shall hear *in the morning*, oh LORD; *in the morning* I will direct it to You, and I will look up" (Psalm 5:3).

"Oh God, You are my God; *early* will I seek You; my soul thirsts for You; my flesh longs for You in a dry and thirsty land where there is no water" (Psalm 63:1).

"But to You I have cried out, oh LORD, and *in the morning* my prayer comes before You" (Psalm 88:13). (See also Psalms 30:5, 46:5, 55:17, 57:8, 59:16.)

Jesus often rose early, before the rising of the sun, to pray and to be alone with the Father. (See Mark 1:35.)

For some people, early morning hours are marvelous. For others, they are disastrous. You must find the time that is best for you, for your lifestyle, your job, your family. The point is to establish a set time and discipline yourself to practice prayer in the school of prayer.

Establish a place of prayer.

Jesus not only rose a great while before day; he departed into a solitary place to pray. Jesus found a place where He could be free of interruptions. In this solitary place, whether it was a desert, mountain or wilderness, Jesus had quality time with the Father. Jesus often retreated to these solitary places at strategic times. (See Matthew 14:23; Luke 22:39-41.)

Find a secluded place away from interruptions, a place where you can assume any prayer posture you desire, a place where you can pray as loud or as quietly as you desire, a place where you can read Scriptures, sing, shout, groan, bind, proclaim, in privacy and solitude.

Establish a prayer plan, procedure and pattern you can follow.

This does not need to be the same, rigid pattern each time you pray. Obviously, the Holy Spirit will lead you through different seasons of prayer. There are advantages to following some basic patterns that have proved beneficial to others. Numerous good books are available on the effective use of your prayer time. Larry Lea's book, *Could You Not Tarry One Hour?* develops the use of the Lord's prayer. Praying this prayer, section by section, easily consumes an hour. Another great prayer plan is presented by Dick Eastman in his book, *The Hour That Changes the World.* The following diagram illustrates his plan for an hour of guided prayer.

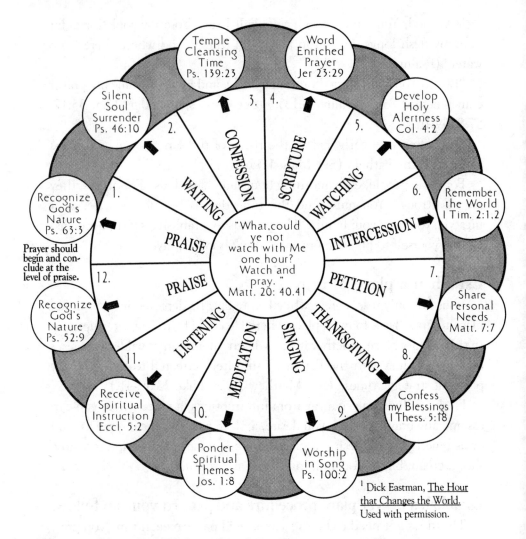

¹ Dick Eastman, The Hour
that Changes the World.
Used with permission.

Entering the School of Intercessory Prayer

The disciplined life of devotional prayer, general petitions and the biblical apostolic prayer are good foundations for moving into a life of intercessory prayer. Intercession moves us from seeking God for our own needs to seeking God for the particular needs of others. Intercession moves the prayer into a hedge-building, protective and warring prayer for others. Intercession is moving into the gap for other's salvation, healing, deliverance, a turning point in a crisis. This is a level of praying in which all believers can function as the Holy Spirit graces them to do so.

Although I do not see intercession or intercessory prayer as a New Testament spiritual gift given only to a select few, I do see certain people who develop the ministry of intercessory prayer more than others, as they are motivated to learn, discipline their time and become equipped in the school of intercessory prayer. They will obviously do it more often, more deeply and with more results. The skills learned and applied will mature the desirous intercessor. In Luke 2:37, Anna, a widow, served God in the temple with fasting and prayer night and day. It could be said that Anna gave herself to the ministry of intercession. The Scripture does not imply that she had a special gift.

As you begin to give yourself to more prayer, you will desire to pray more. As you develop the art of intercession, you will find yourself interceding more. Learn all you can and give yourself to this type of praying as often as possible. The whole Church, all believers, can enjoy corporate prayer-intercession, small-group intercession, personal times of intercession, and some will desire to develop specialized intercession.

We have endeavored to establish the awesome power of Spirit-led and Spirit-filled intercession. Thank you for reading this book and for becoming one of God's faithful intercessors. Together we have journeyed and we have learned.

- We are living in a unique season of spiritual opportunity. God has given us a window to shape history through intercessory prayer.
- Our nation and many nations of the world are at a historical and spiritual crossroads. Our hope and future is in the hands of intercessory prayer.
- Generation X and following generations can become, and will become, "Generations of Destiny." Through intercessory prayer we can capture this generation for God.
- Intercessory prayer is for every believer in every nation, every city, every church. No one is excused.
- Intercessory prayer has awesome power to move God's hand to show mercy instead of judgement and healing instead of destruction.
- Intercessory prayer stands in the gap, rebuilds the spiritual hedges and fills the prayer cup in heaven.
- Every church must become an interceding church, with Holy Spirit power to penetrate the gates of hell and bring down spiritual strongholds.

We are in the mist of one of the greatest prayer revivals in the history of the Christian Church. Never has there been more prayer by more people in more places than now. God is raising up interceding leaders who will motivate interceding people to build interceding churches that will affect cities, regions and nations.

Dr. Peter Wagner writes, "A prayer movement that greatly surpasses anything like it in living memory, perhaps in all of Christian history, is rapidly gaining momentum." This is a *kairos* movement in history, a moment of destiny. *Kairos*, the Greek word for "time," characterizes the content and the quality of the time period. It is a significant moment made significant by a divine encounter with God. *Kairos* is a prophetic season, a season of spiritual opportunity, a window in God's timetable.

We stand at a spiritual and historical crossroads. God moves, creates circumstances, raises up leaders and deals with people as He seeks to fulfill appointed crossroads of history. As we pray and discern God's dealings and God's time clock, we may intersect with divine appointment, resulting in a *kairos* moment in our lives. What a time to be alive, to be a believer and to be moved on by God to join the prayer army around the world! With the Psalmist, let us all pray and proclaim, "It is time for you to act, oh Lord" (Psalm 119:126). May this *kairos* time be made possible through a people who discern the season of intercession!

Further Study

1. Why is it important to make an intercessory prayer covenant? What can we learn from scripture concerning the making of such a covenant?

2. What steps will help you become more committed to intercessory prayer?

3. Is prayer something that happens naturally or does it require some hard work and personal discipline? Explain.

Note

1. Dick Eastman, <u>The Hour that Changes the World</u> (Baker Books, 1978) 136. Used with permission.

Appendix

Appendix

Appendix A:
Pastoral Suggestions From City Bible Church

I have included here, in short form, some ideas and thoughts on how City Bible Church has incorporated prayer-intercession into corporate church services. I pray these ideas and suggestions will encourage leaders and pastors to move out further and deeper in the area of prayer-intercession for their congregations, cities, and nations.

Objectives for Prayer-Intercessors

If a person desires to be involved with specialized intercession, there are certain qualifications to be satisfied. Anyone can participate in corporate church intercession, but training is needed to participate in other levels of intercession that involve privileged information, warfare and time commitment. The following are some basic qualifications we use:

- Must be a committed church member
- Must have completed or be currently taking our church membership class
- Must be faithful in church attendance
- Must be faithful in tithing
- Must be loyal and submissive to the church leadership
- Must not be a gossip
- Must be easily adjusted
- Must not be carrying his or her own agenda
- Must be willing to be trained and attend any intercessory training offered by the church leadership

- Must have his or her personal life in order
- Must have a consistent life of holiness
- Must be properly related to the church, spouse, family and other relationships in the church
- Must have a good report inside and outside of the church
- Must be an individual of faith
- Must have a consistent, daily, personal prayer life
- Must participate in corporate prayer times (pre-service prayer and special prayer meetings)

Areas of Interest

Specialized intercession may be broken down into the following categories.

General Intercession

These individuals have identified themselves and desire more training and a commitment to gathering with other general intercessors for intercession. These pray-ers agree to intercede faithfully for the local church and the leaders of the church. General intercessors receive a weekly or monthly updated prayer intercessory report to help them pray specifically and effectively for the specified areas. They are also on alert for special emergencies in the church or on the mission field. This group meets together once a month for equipping and intercession.

Strategic Group Intercessors

These intercessors meet weekly to intercede for a specific ministry of the local church. This can be itemized according to the function of each specific local church.

Ours would look something like this:

- Group 1: Children's ministry, elementary school, junior high and high school and the leaders of these ministries
- Group 2: Evangelism, ministries to downtown, inner city, young adults, single adults, and the leaders of these ministries
- Group 3: Portland Bible College, publishing department, tape department, Ministers Fellowship International and the leaders of these departments

- Group 4: Pastoral districts, families, older singles, senior saints and the leaders of these groups
- Group 5: Civil government–national, state, county and city
- Group 6: Pastor Frank and his family, along with elders and their families
- Group 7: Administration–facilities, financial, custodial, maintenance, press and pastoral departments
- Group 8: Music department, worship services and the leaders of these ministries
- Group 9: Healing needs of the church

Healing and Deliverance Intercession Teams

These prayer teams will specialize in ministering to people who have specific needs for healing or deliverance. The people needing prayer will meet with these groups on an appointment basis on Tuesday and Thursday nights in the prayer center. To make an appointment they call the church office and a time is arranged to meet with the intercessors.

Corporate Service Intercession Teams

There are two different groups of public service intercessors. One group meets during the actual church service and intercedes for that service. This group will intercede for God to do mighty works in that worship service, through that particular preacher and for that particular altar call. These intercessors usually intercede for two and a half hours. Another group of intercessors meets together in the sanctuary before the service to pray over every chair, every pew, every instrument, every door, the pulpit, etc. They intercede for God's blessing and favor to be in that room for that day or service.

Personal Prayer-intercession Teams

These intercessors pray for individual leaders in the church. These intercessors are invited by the leader desiring intercession to be one of a team of intercessors. This leader will communicate his or her needs to the intercessors, who will then make constant intercession on the leader's behalf. The leader usually meets with his or her personal intercessors on a weekly basis.

Prayer Center

We also have a prayer center on our campus that is open from six o'clock in the morning until ten o'clock in the evening, seven days a week.

Many of our trained intercessors are on assignment in the prayer center. It is also open for all church members, every day. This has been another way to focus on intercessory prayer and give prayer a place on our campus.

Appendix B:
An Introduction to Service Prayer Teams

The Purpose of Service Prayer Teams

"But when He saw the multitudes, He was moved with compassion for them, because they were weary and scattered, like sheep having no shepherd. Then He said to His disciples, 'The harvest truly is plentiful, but the laborers are few. Therefore pray the Lord of the harvest to send out laborers into His harvest' " (Matthew 9:36-38).

Certainly those who are lost need prayer more than those who know the Lord. But Jesus said, "The workers are few." Where do the workers come from? It has been my observation (and I believe confirmed by scriptures like Ephesians 4:11-12 and Hebrews 10:24-25) that most of the workers come as a result of God moving in a corporate service.

Consider your own life. Have not most of the inspiration, instruction and opportunity for productive kingdom activity come as a result of the corporate meeting? I suspect that without corporate meetings, there would be virtually no laborers. Even though that is the case, do we really need "intercessory prayer" for our services, especially when the Holy Spirit is already moving in an awesome way?

Lord, Please Do More

The research of C. Peter Wagner, a respected scholar on prayer, reveals that we are in the midst of the greatest prayer movement in world history. Most Christian leaders credit the present outpouring of the Spirit to prayer. Marvelous things are happening as a result. But I am not satisfied, are you? Let us go to the next level—*but it's going to take prayer.* That is why the church leadership is so excited about the Service Prayer Teams. It WILL make a difference. Here are just some of the tremendous things God is doing in our services. Lord, please do more.

Salvation	Physical and emotional healing
Personal renewal	Relationships established and restored
Marriages strengthened	Commitments to holy living
Calling of God	Repentance
Teaching	Response of the heart
Impartation	Counseling and guidance
Ministry to the youth	Financial giving

Suggestions On How To Pray For Services

Naturally, there are as many ways to pray as there are Christians, but here are some brief guidelines that might be helpful.

- *Enjoy the worship service.* Even though you are going to spend much of the service in prayer, feel free to participate in worship. Most Service Prayer Teams will go to the staff conference room to pray at offering time.

- *Cooperate with the purpose of God.* God has a number of strategic purposes for every service. For example, one thing He seems to be doing right now is increasing our faith for a release of divine healing. Let your prayers encourage what He is doing. God also has a specific purpose for each individual in attendance. You may know a friend or family member with a special need, a note may be sent in from the service requesting prayer for a visiting pastor or missionary or the Holy Spirit may move you to intercede for someone you do not even know.

- *Cooperate with the Holy Spirit.* Romans 8:26-27 states that we often do not know how to pray (I know the feeling). Fortunately, the Holy Spirit can intercede through us. In fact, the verse goes on to say that the Holy Spirit's intercessions may come in ways that cannot be expressed in words. Be led by the Spirit and feel free to pray in tongues.

- **_Cooperate with the team leader._** For continuity, communication purposes and safety, a leader has been appointed for each Service Prayer Team. We believe each of these leaders to be mature in the Lord. Each leader also has a degree of liberty in how they structure the prayer time. If it turns out that their particular prayer structure is not exactly your preferred style, please go with the flow. God will be pleased with your flexibility and has promised to bless those who walk in unity and agreement.

Appendix C:
Prayer and Praise Service Agendas

Sample Agenda A: Prayer and Praise Service

"Prayer That Releases and Receives the Rain of God"

- Opening Chorus

- Corporate Prayer Time (short, dedicating service to God)

- Chorus: "I Will Never Be The Same Again"

- Prayer

- Word on Prayer and Rain

- Sections of Prayer

    1. Rain and Repentance: teach on repentance – lead in repentance prayer

    2. Rain and Renewal: chorus–"*Spirit, Touch Your Church*"

    3. Rain on Our City and Region: chorus–"*Lord, We Pray for Our City*"

    4. Rain of God's Presence

5. Rain and Prosperity

6. Rain and Harvest: chorus–"*Let Your Glory Fall In This Place*"

- Announcements

- Offering

- Dismiss Children

- Worship

- Ministry Time

This agenda is subject to the moving of the Holy Spirit!

Sample Agenda B: Prayer and Praise Service

"Envisioning Our Future"

- Corporate Prayer

- Water Baptisms

- Scripture Reading

- Six Sections of Prayer

    1. City Strongholds   *Pastor Frank Damazio*

    2. House of Healing and Miracles   *Larry Asplund*

    3. Increase in Growth and Harvest   *Pastor Frank Damazio*
        - Return of the Prodigal   *Ed Schefter*
        - Reaching the Homosexual Community   *James Monaghan*
        - Reaching Generation X   *Steve Trujillo*

4. Raising Up Intercessors   *Bob MacGregor*
   • Prayer Over Intercessors   *Pastor Frank Damazio*

5. Financial Blessing   *Howard Rachinski*

6. New Release of the Spirit Upon the Women *Libby Louman*

• Worship

• Ministry Time

Sample Agenda C: Congretional Handout

PRAYER AND PRAISE SUNDAY
A Time to Soak, Receive, Be Refreshed!

Pastor Frank Damazio

INTRODUCTION: Today we specifically set aside our morning service to focus on praying and receiving. The flow of the service will be a little different than our normal Sunday service. Today we will read scriptures and move together as a church into prayer times. Please relax and enjoy these times of prayer. Some of the service will be led from the platform and some will be in small groups of people praying and ministering to one another. No one will be asked to pray or minister; it will be voluntary and spontaneous. We will, after a season of prayer ministry, break for offering and announcements and then move into an extended time of praise and worship. There will not be the normal sermon time, but I will be giving scriptures and thoughts throughout the service. This is a day to soak in God's presence. Be refreshed. Be encouraged. Be filled with God's Spirit. Let us enter in with faith and rejoicing.

The Praying Church
Isaiah 56:7

Hodge: Prayer should be the breath of our breathing, the thought of our thinking, the soul of our feeling and the life of our living, the sound of our hearing, the growth of our growing.

Wesley: You need not utterly despair even of those who for the present turn again and rend you. For if all your arguments and persuasiveness fail, there is yet another remedy left and one that is frequently found effectual when no other method avails. This is prayer! Therefore whatever you desire or want, either for others or for your own soul, ask and it shall be given you.

Samuel Chadwick: Satan dreads nothing but prayer. . . .The church that lost its Christ was full of good works. The one concern of the devil is to keep the saints from praying. . . .He laughs at our toil, mocks at our wisdom, but trembles when we pray.

Prayer and the Church in the Book of Acts

1. Acts 1:13-14	7. Acts 8:14-15,22,24-25
2. Acts 1:24	8. Acts 9:5-6,11; 22:8-18; 26:12-19
3. Acts 3:1	9. Acts 9:36-43
4. Acts 4:23,31	10. Acts 10:2-4,9,30-31,48
5. Acts 6:4,7	11. Acts 12:5,12-17
6. Acts 7:55-60	12. Acts 13:2-3,43

I. PERSONAL PRAYER AND THE BELIEVER
Psalm 51:1-13

A. Prayer for God's graciousness, lovingkindness and compassion
Psalm 51:1

B. Prayer for God to wash and cleanse me from my transgressions
Psalm 51:2-10

C. Prayer for God to renew and restore my Spirit

Psalm 51:10-13

D. Prayer for God to give me a broken and contrite heart

Psalm 51:17

II. PERSONAL PRAISE AND THE BELIEVER

Psalm 51:14-19

A. Experiencing the awesome presence of God

Psalm 51:8, 11

B. Experiencing the freedom of expressing your praise

Psalm 51:14-15

C. Exalting God with the sacrifice of praise

Psalm 51:16-17, 19

D. Expecting God to do good to His people

Psalm 51:18

Leader to Leader Training

Seasons of Revival
Frank Damazio

Seasons of Revival offers fresh insight in understanding God's seasons of outpouring. The truths presented will enable you to enjoy greater refreshing during this season of revival.
ISBN 1-886849-03-X

The Making of a Leader
Frank Damazio

This bestseller presents a scriptual analysis of the philosophy, history, qualifications and practice of Christian leadership. You will be challenged by the illustrations from the life of David and others.
ISBN 0-914936-84-0

Timothy Training Program
Frank Damazio

How does a pastor keep up with all the demands of building a church? The *Timothy Training Program* will provide the tools for training new leaders.
Teachers 0-914936-12-3
Students 0-914936-13-1

Covenants
Kevin Conner

Covenants gives a biblical framework for understanding the administration of God's dealings with mankind throught human history.
ISBN 0-914936-77-8

Worship God!
Ernest Gentile

Worship God! is exhaustive on the subject of worship with answers to understanding and enjoying spiritually vital worship.
ISBN 0-914936-06-9

Eternity: The Ultimate Choice
Marc Estes

This cutting edge booklet approaches from a fresh veiwpoint the question of eternity, the authenticity of the Bible and the gospel message.
ISBN 1-886849-07-2

Ask for these resources at your local Christian bookstore.

BT Publishing is a ministry of
City Bible Church in Portland, Oregon.
Call 1-800-777-6057 for a complete catalog.